JAPANESE BUDDHISM

JAPANESE BUDDHISM
A Cultural History

by

Yoshiro Tamura

translated by

Jeffrey Hunter

KOSEI PUBLISHING CO. • *Tokyo*

The contents of this book were originally published in Japanese by Kosei Publishing Co. in the January–December 1967 issues of the monthly magazine *Yakushin*, under the series title "Hyakuman Nin no Bukkyō-shi" (A History of Japanese Buddhism for a Million Readers). The series was published in book form by Kadokawa Shoten in 1969 under the title *Nihon Bukkyō-shi Nyūmon* (An Introductory History of Japanese Buddhism).

Shown on the front and back covers is the frontispiece and the beginning of the text of chapter 14 of the Lotus Sutra, "A Happy Life," from the *Heikenōkyō*, a historic set of thirty-three scrolls of copied sutras. The Siddham ideogram on a disk represents Shakyamuni, the historical Buddha. The set was dedicated by Taira no Kiyomori and his clan in 1164 to the deity of Itsukushima Shrine in what is now Hiroshima Prefecture. Designated a National Treasure of Japan. Owned by Itsukushima Shrine. Photograph courtesy of the Nara National Museum.

Cover design by NOBU. The text of this book is set in a computer version of Monotype Baskerville with a computer version of Optima for display.

First English edition, 2000
Third printing, 2005

Published by Kosei Publishing Co., 2-7-1 Wada, Suginami-ku, Tokyo 166-8535, Japan. Copyright © 1967, 1969 by Yoshiro Tamura, 2000 by Kosei Publishing Co.; all rights reserved.

ISBN 4-333-01684-3

Contents

Preface

JAPAN IS OFTEN DESCRIBED as having a hybrid culture. But this does not mean that disparate cultural elements were simply embraced indiscriminately; rather, they were vigorously assimilated and skillfully made over into Japanese cultural artifacts. The same thing happened with Buddhism: It was absorbed into Japanese culture and reconstituted as Japanese Buddhism. Thus it is impossible to separate Japan's Buddhism from the nation's cultural matrix, or to explicate the one without understanding the other.

Japanese scholars have produced some fine histories of Japanese Buddhism. Most of these works, however, confine themselves to historical facts and make use only of purely Buddhist sources. Few discuss such literary classics as the *Man'yōshū*, *Genji monogatari*, *Hōjōki*, and *Tsurezuregusa*, though it is impossible to grasp the distinctive features of Japanese Buddhism without some knowledge of these works. Conversely, Japan's literary scholars tend to disregard or show only a cursory interest in Buddhism. This, too, precludes true understanding of Japanese literature. Some literary works are so deeply steeped in Buddhism that they can justly be considered Buddhist writings, but they are ignored by Buddhist scholars, while literary scholars discuss Japanese literature as though Buddhism did not exist. This blinkered approach distorts both fields of scholarship.

Traditionally, historians have applied historical methodology to the study of Japanese Buddhism. That has become the mainstream approach, one that focuses on what we might call the outer history. I have chosen to approach the subject from the inside, as it were, by writing an intellectual history of Japanese Buddhism. This has meant examining Japanese Buddhism in the context of literary and intellectual trends, as well as of other religions. For this reason I have devoted a great deal of space to literary works and to other religions—Shintō, folk religion, Christianity, new religions—while omitting some of the details of strictly Buddhist developments.

Since this book represents an approach to Japanese culture and thought, nothing would make me happier than to have it read as an introduction to Japan's cultural and intellectual history.

Editorial Note

IN THIS BOOK all Japanese personal names follow the customary Japanese name order: family name followed by given name. As a rule, premodern figures are referred to by given name on second and subsequent mentions, whereas modern figures are referred to by surname. The transition from premodern to modern is the Meiji era (1868–1912). In the case of transitional figures, the name used tends to reflect the time at which the person was most active or with which he or she is most closely identified.

Macrons, indicating sustained vowels, are used where appropriate with all Japanese names and terms except in the case of the cities of Tokyo (Tōkyō), Kyoto (Kyōto), and Osaka (Ōsaka). A modified orthography that does not include diacritical marks is used for Sanskrit names and terms. The Wade-Giles system is followed in the transliteration of Chinese names and terms.

Every effort has been made to adhere to the Western method of reckoning people's age. (The traditional Japanese method includes the year of birth, so that on one's first birthday one is considered to be two years old, not one year old.) Some anomalies may remain, however, since it has proved impossible to verify all the ages mentioned in the original Japanese text.

JAPANESE BUDDHISM

CHAPTER ONE

Early Japan and
the Arrival of Buddhism

NATIONS CAN NO LONGER exist independent of one another. The economic and political activities of one nation can no longer be isolated from those of others, and cultural and intellectual exchange is rapidly increasing. The internationalization of information, spurred by satellite communications, means that for the first time in history cultures the world over are in direct contact. We are on the threshold of a period of great cross-fertilization.

In Japan, this has meant not only a continued and increasing closeness with the cultures of the West, a process that began in the mid-nineteenth century, but also a new opening up toward other Asian nations, as well as the cultures of Africa and the Middle East. With Japan's growing role on the international stage, its culture and thought are finding advocates in other nations, opening new avenues of expression for their own cultures.

Ukiyo-e woodblock prints and Zen Buddhism are two Japanese cultural elements that enjoy international appreciation. *Ukiyo-e* influenced Edgar Degas and Vincent van Gogh, providing European painting with new inspiration in the mid- and late nineteenth century. Zen Buddhism, meanwhile, has offered Western spiritual seekers a means to go beyond the confines of Christianity and existentialist philosophy. Many other elements of Japanese culture and thought have piqued the interest of Westerners, who have begun

13

to study aspects of Japanese culture that fill gaps in the Western tradition.

There is no point, however, in emphasizing such dichotomies as Eastern versus Western philosophy or Japanese versus non-Japanese thought. It is time for us to transcend these categories and, from an international viewpoint based upon exchange among all nations, consider a single culture, a single history of thought. As far as philosophy and religion are concerned, the division between East and West has been overcome. This is what the great German philosopher Karl Jaspers meant when he stated that we are at the stage where a world philosophy must be established.

Nevertheless, however universal our concerns, we must not ignore the unique qualities of each nation and people and paint the globe a dull, homogeneous gray. Rather, we must allow the individuality of each nation and people to flourish on the larger stage of international culture. While channeling the distinctive streams of national cultures into the great sea of international culture, we must also allow the current of international culture to augment individual cultures. The history of Japanese Buddhism provides an excellent example of just such a process.

Buddhism, Christianity, and Islam are the three great world religions. Though Buddhism originated in India, it soon spread to the east, acquiring an international cast. Japan's national character and physical setting have colored Japanese culture and thought. It is widely recognized that Japan has adopted much from foreign sources, but it is just as widely recognized that the Japanese have not been satisfied with simple imitation but have adapted their borrowings, thus enriching their own culture.

Borrowings aside, it is clear that Japan has distinctive patterns of culture and thought. It was, in fact, the existence of basic underlying patterns that made the skillful assimilation of non-Japanese thought and culture possible, and their combination into a peculiarly Japanese blend inevitable. When we explore the history of Japanese Buddhism, then, we discover how the universal spirit of Buddhism stretched the bounds of the Japanese people's experience and, at the same time, how the Japanese digested Buddhism and what kind of Buddhism resulted. I would like to begin this exploration by reviewing briefly the route along which Buddhism traveled to Japan.

Shakyamuni, the historical Buddha, lived in India in about the fifth century before the common era. The dates of his birth and death are not known, and various dates have traditionally been given, but recent research suggests two probabilities: the Buddha lived either from 560 to 480 or from 460 to 380. If we accept the earlier dates, the Buddha lived at the same time as Confucius; if we accept the later ones, Socrates and Lao-tzu were his contemporaries. Though it may be nothing but coincidence, there was tremendous intellectual activity at the time the Buddha lived, particularly in India, where he was one of many philosophical and religious seekers who were considering the nature of humanity and the world from every possible point of view. The profundity of Buddhism as a philosophy and a religion is partly a result of the intellectually challenging age in which it took form.

Many schools of Buddhism arose during the reign of the Indian king Ashoka (ca. 274–ca. 236 B.C.E.). Later they were grouped together and called Hinayana, or the Lesser Vehicle, by reformers who called themselves followers of Mahayana, or the Great Vehicle. The beginnings of Mahayana Buddhism can be traced to the first century of the common era. Its history in India is usually divided into four periods: the first to third century, the fourth century, the fifth and sixth centuries, and the seventh century. After that Indian Buddhism declined and was largely absorbed into popular religious practice and ritual. In 1203 the great Buddhist monastery-university at Vikramashila was destroyed by Muslim invaders and for all practical purposes Buddhism disappeared from India. But before its eclipse it had spread to other lands, where it continued to develop.

Buddhism traveled to Japan from China via the Korean Peninsula. There are various theories of the transmission of Buddhism to China. Recent findings suggest that the Indian religion probably reached China through Central Asia around the beginning of the common era. By that time there was considerable cultural and material exchange along the Silk Road. No doubt Buddhism was part of that exchange. That China had already expanded its territory to include parts of Central Asia strongly suggests that it was Central Asian rather than Indian Buddhism that was first known to the Chinese. Thus early Chinese Buddhism was not a direct offshoot of Indian Buddhism but was a Central Asian development of the Indian teaching.

Direct contact between China and Indian Buddhism began during the Eastern Chin dynasty (317–420), when the first Indian priests arrived in China and Chinese priests began to travel to India to study the religion. Buddhism was transmitted from China to the Korean Peninsula in 372, when China's ruler sent a Chinese priest and Buddhist scriptures and images to the northern Korean kingdom of Koguryŏ. In 384 the Indian priest Malananda sailed from China to Paekche, a kingdom on the southwestern coast of the Korean Peninsula. The religion was transmitted from Koguryŏ to the southeastern kingdom of Silla in the fifth century. The ruler of Silla greatly encouraged the new religion, and Korean priests were sent to China and even to India to study it.

The official transmission of Buddhism to Japan took place in the sixth century, when King Syŏngmyŏng of Paekche sent an envoy bearing an image and scriptures to the Japanese court. The traditional date for this transmission is 552, but 538 is the currently accepted date. Though this year marked the official introduction of Buddhism, it had actually entered Japan earlier on a private basis, as Chinese Buddhists who lived on the Korean Peninsula emigrated to Japan. The twelfth-century *Fusō ryakki* [Abridged Annals of Japan], for example, mentions that in 522 the Chinese Ssu-ma Tateng (known in Japan as Shiba Tatto) emigrated to Japan, where he built a hut in which he installed a Buddhist image. His daughter Shimame took Buddhist vows in 584 and adopted the Buddhist name Zenshinni. She was the first person to be ordained in Japan and was followed by his son Tasuna, who took the Buddhist name Tokusai.

Shiba Tatto's grandson Kuratsukuri no Tori (known as Tori Busshi, or "Buddhist sculptor Tori") was regarded in later ages as the father of Japanese Buddhist sculpture. Among the works attributed to him is the Shakyamuni triad (Shakyamuni flanked by two bodhisattvas) in the temple Hōryū-ji, in Nara. Clearly, the transmission to Japan of Buddhism, and of continental culture and technology in general, owed a great deal to immigrants. From the fifth through the seventh century, many Chinese and Koreans settled in Japan and were active in a wide variety of fields. Their descendants formed important clans that played a great role in the nation's development.

When considering the development of Buddhism in Japan, we must always ask ourselves how Buddhism responded to the pre-Buddhist Japanese way of thinking and how the Japanese perceived and assimilated Buddhism. In the course of Buddhism's long travels from India through Central Asia to China and on to the Korean Peninsula, it adapted to a variety of civilizations and was modified by the various peoples who adopted it. Yet a common Buddhist spirit or way of thinking remained as a strong undercurrent, nourishing and guiding each of these developments. Our question is whether, upon arriving at its final destination in East Asia, Japan, this common undercurrent of the Buddhist spirit continued to flow. In other words, was Buddhism in Japan completely Japanized, transformed into a unique religion different in essence from original Buddhism?

The way of thinking that developed as a result of Japan's historical and geographical circumstances is tenacious; moreover, Buddhism arrived in Japan as a fully developed, cohesive system with a great volume of scriptures and commentaries. Japan, which already had its own patterns of culture and thought, was faced with all the paraphernalia of a great world religion. To learn what these patterns were, we must review the nation's origins and the first traces of Japanese culture and thought.

The first evidence of culture in Japan dates from the New Stone Age, known in Japan as the Jōmon (rope pattern) period (ca. 10,000–300 B.C.E.), so called after the earthenware marked with twisted-rope patterns that has been discovered from that time. Recent archaeological research has been turning up more and more information on the Old Stone Age, but as yet not enough is known to allow us to speculate on the cultural patterns of the Japanese at that time. Japanese history begins, then, with the cultural patterns of the Jōmon period.

The New Stone Age in Europe was characterized by the use of polished stone implements, the production of pottery, and the beginnings of agriculture and animal husbandry. While the first two elements are also evident in Japan's Jōmon period, the Japanese continued to live by hunting and gathering. Thus there were no crops to be stored, and there was no accumulation of wealth; as a consequence, social classes did not arise, nor did social groups form around authority figures. A low social consciousness and undeveloped material civilization were characteristics that remained with Japanese society for some time. That does not mean, however, that the Japanese were "primitive." Indeed, these very characteristics have sometimes proved Japan's greatest assets. The long dependence of the Japanese people on hunting and gathering is what made them so responsive to the natural world and led to the development of such rich aesthetic and emotional vocabularies.

In order to learn of the religious beliefs of the Jōmon period, we must refer to such artifacts as clay figures (*dogū*) and stone rods and to burial customs. Most *dogū* are figures of women with large breasts and bellies. Scholars differ in their interpretation of the meaning of the figures. It has been suggested that they were fertility images that embodied prayers for abundance of the plant and animal life upon which the Jōmon people depended for food. It has also been surmised that the preponderance of female images indicates that women enjoyed high social status. Many of the stone rods that have been found are in the shape of phalluses. Some scholars believe that the rods were indeed intended to represent phalluses, whereas others hold that they were simply tools for digging. But stone rods so large that they could have had no practical use support the opinion that they served some sort of ritual function.

Many of the dead from this period were buried in the fetal position, and in some cases large stones and earthenware implements were placed on their heads and stomachs. Four theories of the meaning of this burial practice are current: that the stones prevented the spirits of the dead from leaving their graves and harming the living; that the fetal position was intended to ensure rebirth; that this position symbolized rest; and, finally, the practical consideration that this position permitted the deceased to be buried in a grave that required little digging. Some scholars also suggest that the Jōmon-period shell mounds that have been found in various parts of Japan were simply middens, whereas others believe that they served the additional purpose of sending the spirits of the eaten shellfish back to the heavens, with prayers that they would return to the earth and enrich people's lives again.

It is difficult to draw general conclusions about the meaning of artifacts thousands of years old, but several hypotheses have been suggested. One is that people of the time perceived a spiritual power in certain objects and phenomena. This power was feared for the harm it could cause and was prayed to and propitiated for the benefits it could bestow. This kind of religious belief is called animism, which, described simply, is worship of nature and belief in nature spirits. Animism was the natural outgrowth of the conditions of life in prehistoric times, when people were completely dependent upon the vagaries of the natural world.

It is fascinating to note that animism has remained part of the Japanese religious tradition down to the present. Buddhism rejects animism in principle, but the current of animist belief runs so strongly and continuously through Japanese culture that Buddhism was influenced by it almost immediately upon its introduction to Japan. This is one manifestation of the Japanization of Buddhism. The persistence of animistic beliefs in Japan leads some people to infer that the Japanese religious consciousness is undeveloped. It is the ancient inclination of the Japanese to live in close accord with nature, pointed out above, that has sustained animistic worship of nature to modern times. But to conclude from this alone that Japanese religious consciousness or thought is undeveloped is premature.

The long Jōmon period was followed by the Yayoi period, which is regarded as having begun in 300 B.C.E. and is subdivided into early (300–100 B.C.E.), middle (100 B.C.E.–100 C.E.), and late (100–

300 C.E.). With the introduction of wet rice cultivation and bronze and iron implements from the Asian continent, Yayoi culture took an immense leap forward. Yet stone tools continued in use. Most early civilizations progressed from the Old Stone Age through the New Stone Age into the Bronze and Iron ages, shedding the artifacts of the previous era as they moved into the next. In Japan, however, old and new remained in use side by side. Modern Japanese culture is often described as a medium where new and old coexist. This tendency was already observable, it seems, in the Yayoi period.

Wet rice cultivation encouraged the development of permanent communities, for rice cultivation is practical only as a group effort and ties the group to the land. With the cultivation of rice in paddies, a surplus of food also became available for the first time, and with surplus food came storage. With the practice of storage, village leaders arose. Eventually small kingdoms were born. Japan in the late Yayoi period is described in contemporary Chinese annals, providing us with a glimpse of life at that crucial stage in the nation's development.

In a chapter titled "The People of Wa," the *Wei chih* [Wei Chronicle], an account of the third-century Wei dynasty of northern China, provides a description of the land of Wa, as Japan was known to the Chinese. Of particular interest is the account of Queen Himiko of the kingdom of Yamatai. It seems that Yamatai was wracked by rebellions for decades, until a woman named Himiko was made its ruler. She was said to be "master of the Way of Demons" and to keep her subjects well in hand. Her younger brother, her main assistant in affairs of state, mediated between the queen and her subjects. A more typically shamanic ruler could not be found. Queen Himiko was a female shaman (*miko* in Japanese), and thus unmarried, who received the communications of the deities and governed accordingly.

Yamatai's location is uncertain. The two dominant theories place it on southwestern Honshū or on northern Kyūshū. Though we lack a more detailed description of life in Yayoi times, it is clear that the feeling of a spiritual presence and power in the natural world and its phenomena governed Japanese life. There was no notion of anthropomorphic deities. Sacred presence and power were perceived instead in mountains and forests, in seas and rivers, in rain, wind, and lightning, and sometimes in animals and plants. The manifestations of that presence and power were designated and worshiped as _kami_, a word closer in meaning to _mana_ than to _god_. In their village councils the Yayoi people sought the advice of the _kami_ and developed various artifacts for calling on the deities. Called _yorishiro_, literally "approach substitutes," these artifacts were designed, like lightning rods, to attract the deities and give them physical objects to occupy.

Quiet sites in the mountains or forests were selected for village councils, and often a great tree or other natural object was selected as the _yorishiro_. These gathering places eventually evolved into the shrines of the nascent (but still nameless) Shintō religion. Hints of the natural origins of shrines can be found in the Japanese words for mountain and forest, which can also mean shrine. The type of Shintō shrine that exists today, with a large worship hall and images, came about as a result of Buddhist influence.

Traces of the pre-Buddhist tradition are evident in a few shrines even today. Ōmiwa Shrine, in Nara, for example, contains no sacred image; the mountain on which the shrine stands is regarded as the deity the shrine serves. Thus while the shrine has a worship hall (_haiden_), it lacks a hall of the deity (_shinden_). Many other shrines have a giant tree girded with a sacred rope (_shimenawa_) in their precincts or enshrine sacred objects, such as a mirror, sword, or jewel (actually a comma-shaped piece of jade). Originally these objects were not deities but _yorishiro_. Only later did they come to be regarded, by association, as deities themselves. The first buildings constructed at shrine sites were no doubt built to house the _yorishiro;_ the term for these "deity storehouses"—_hokura_—evolved into one of the early words for shrine, _hokora_. Later the term _miya_ came into use. _Miya_ means palace, and its use in reference to shrines indicates that shrine buildings had developed from unadorned huts into the ornate edifices we see today.

Several words were used to refer to the divine in ancient times:

chi, mi, tama, mono, and *kami*. <u>*Chi, mi,* and *tama*</u> also appear in various compounds, such as *mizuchi* (water spirit), *orochi* (mountain spirit), *ikazuchi* (thunder), *kunochi* (tree spirit), *nuzuchi* (field spirit), *hayachi* (sudden fierce wind), *kochi* (east wind), *shihotsuchi* (tide spirit), *kagutsuchi* (fire spirit), *tsukiyomi* (moon spirit), *yamatsumi* (mountain spirit), *wadatsumi* (sea spirit), *kodama* (tree spirit), and *kotodama* (word spirit). *Tama* (spirit) points to the typically animist notion of spirits within objects and natural phenomena; *chi* and *mi*, meanwhile, can be traced back to the preanimist stage known as animatism, in which natural phenomena themselves were perceived as awesome existences or beings. *Mono* is believed to have referred to the negative influences or frightening activities of spirits, as the later expression *mononoke* (evil spirit) suggests.

The word *kami* received perhaps its best-known explication at the hands of the great eighteenth-century scholar Motoori Norinaga. In his *Kojiki den,* a commentary on the eighth-century *Kojiki* [Record of Ancient Matters], he defined *kami* as "any thing or phenomenon that produces the emotions of fear and awe, with no distinction between good and evil." *Kami* seems to have been used mainly in connection with objects or phenomena to which either human form or human nature was ascribed.

No clear difference between the Jōmon and Yayoi periods can be identified with regard to religion or views of the divine. But with the stabilization of communities that took place in the Yayoi period, a development in the notion of the divine toward the end of the period is suggested by the fact that *kami* that were leaders of human society began to evolve. In other words, *kami* began to take on human form and characteristics. This became even clearer in the <u>Kofun, or Tumulus, period (300–646)</u>, during which Buddhism was introduced to Japan. That first encounter between the Japanese *kami* and the Buddha, which took place against a backdrop of political struggle, was a historic confrontation between ideas and faiths from which many fascinating developments were to emerge.

CHAPTER TWO

The Birth of the Japanese Nation and the Ascent of Buddhism

THE KOFUN PERIOD is often divided into the early Kofun period, extending from 300 to 450, and the late Kofun period, extending from 450 to 646. The period is so named because its beginning was marked by the construction of giant keyhole-shaped burial mounds, or tumuli (*kofun*), which are thought to indicate the emergence of rulers of a unified Japanese nation. The land of Yamatai mentioned in the earlier *Wei chih*, by contrast, was a local kingdom.

No further mention of Japan is found in Chinese records until the middle of the fifth century, when an entry titled "The Land of Wa" appears in the *Sung shu*, a history of the Liu-Sung dynasty (420–79). This land of Wa appears to have been not a local kingdom but a nation-state.

The enormous burial mounds of the emperors Ōjin (traditional reign dates 269–310) and Nintoku (traditional reign dates 310–99), in present Osaka Prefecture, are representative examples of the massive keyhole-shaped burial mounds that served as symbols of the power and centralized authority of the early national rulers of Japan. The Nintoku Mausoleum, the largest tumulus in Japan, is 475 meters in length; it is estimated that five thousand laborers would have had to work every day for a year to build it. The imperial rule of that time, however, seems to have been not a codified system of government but rather a natural evolution from earlier patterns, and the authority of the ruler had strong mythical and religious overtones. A regime of this sort, unbound by law or code, would naturally change with the changing structure of society. Such a change occurred in the latter half of the period.

With the increasing sophistication of agriculture in the mid-fifth century, the organization of kinship groups headed by patriarchal leaders was encouraged to manage the intensive cooperative labor that the cultivation of rice requires. These groups developed into extended families, or "houses" (*kazoku*), and clans (*shizoku* or *uji*) made up of related families. As a result, the nation evolved into a federation of powerful clans, the emperor being the leader of the strongest clan.

Religious practices changed to adapt to changing social structures. The tombs of the late Kofun period, for example, are very different from the great mausoleums of the early period. Instead of enormous tombs for individual rulers, in the late Kofun period we find many smaller family tombs in various parts of Japan. And whereas the great mausoleums had a single entrance that was sealed up once the deceased had been entombed, these family tombs consisted of chambers with access through side entrances so that family members could be entombed over the years.

The emergence of clans encouraged other new religious developments. Each clan chose a patron deity as its symbol and protector, to be worshiped as the clan's heroic leader and, sometimes, its divine ancestor. These were the clan *kami* (*uji-gami*) that were to play such an important part in later Japanese history. The deities of Japan began to acquire a new overlay of personality. Originally the *kami* had been natural spirits; now they took on a degree of human persona. It was at this pivotal stage that Buddhism was introduced to Japan and the indigenous *kami* and the Buddha first met. But before we look at that fateful encounter, we must explore in more detail Japan's indigenous religion and its stage of development.

We have seen that the early Japanese saw the divine in natural forces and thus felt no need to shape images of the divine or, for the most part, erect permanent halls of worship. Even when a hall for a deity—a *shinden*—was built, it usually housed a *yorishiro*, such as a mirror or a comma-shaped piece of jade called *tama* (jewel) or *magatama* (curved jewel), an artifact to call down the deity and provide the divine spirit with an object to occupy. This practice continued for many centuries. A ninth-century catalogue of the objects of worship enshrined at forty-nine middle- and lower-ranking shrines affiliated with Ise Grand Shrine, sacred to the solar deity, Amaterasu Ōmikami (Great Heaven-Illuminating Deity), mythical progenitor of the imperial line, lists twenty-seven enshrining stones, five enshrining mirrors, one enshrining water, and sixteen with no object of worship. Today, Shintō shrines enshrining mirrors are found throughout Japan.

As clan *kami* became more prominent and took on human attributes, we might expect images in human form to begin to appear in the shrines, but this was not the case. The earliest Shintō image in human form, Sōgyō Hachiman (the *kami* Hachiman in the form of a Buddhist priest), dates no earlier than the tenth century and is obviously strongly Buddhist in character. The paucity of significant Shintō statuary was due to the fact that the Japanese had no concept of a transcendent deity but regarded the divine and the human as dwelling on the same plane. A human being could actually be a *kami* (an *arahito-gami*, or "manifest *kami*," such as the emperor was believed to be); no need was felt to create a separate kind of divine image. Later, when a universal creator *kami*, Musubi no Kami, was included in the Shintō pantheon, the word *musubi* was written with the ideogram meaning birth. This identification of creation with the natural function of birth contrasts sharply with the Christian concept of a transcendental deity standing above nature as creator of the universe.

In general, the Japanese affirm the world and humanity as they are and do not seek a realm or a state of existence that rejects or transcends the natural world. Several reasons can be given for this mindset. For one thing, though there have been many prolonged and bloody contests for power and authority among the Japanese, the nation was never successfully invaded or ruled by another people before the twentieth century, so that the Japanese never had to face the bitter reality of occupation by a foreign power or submission to foreign beliefs. For another, Japan's climate is temperate, and the country has no vast spaces for people to wander in. The Japanese tendency to remain firmly grounded in the natural world has been at times a strength, at times a weakness. This was the environment of thought, feeling, and belief into which Buddhism was introduced, a religion that rejects reality as it is—the phenomenal world—and teaches a way to transcend it.

When Japan's indigenous religion and Buddhism, so different in basic nature, met head on, we would have expected considerable mutual opposition and resistance. According to the eighth-century *Nihon shoki* [Chronicles of Japan], also known as the *Nihongi*, Emperor Kimmei (r. 531–71) received an image of the Buddha and scriptures from an emissary of the king of Paekche in 552. He promptly sought the advice of his councilors on whether the new "*kami*" should be worshiped. Soga no Iname, the leader of one of the great clans of the time, replied that there was no reason for Japan to refuse to accept a religion that was followed in many countries. But the leader of the rival Mononobe clan, Mononobe no Okoshi, opposed acceptance of the foreign faith, proclaiming that "the *kami* of our land will be offended if we worship a foreign *kami*." This was the beginning of bitter conflict between the pro-Buddhist and anti-Buddhist factions at the imperial court, a conflict that gave rise to many dramatic legends telling of the punishments that the indigenous *kami* inflicted on the Soga clan for adopting the foreign religion or, alternatively, of the calamities that befell the Mononobe for scorning Buddhism.

What is most striking about the initial confrontation of the two religions, however, is Mononobe no Okoshi's referring to the Buddha as "a foreign *kami*." He perceived the Buddha as a deity of the same kind as the Japanese *kami*, albeit one belonging to a foreign people. Thus the struggle between the two factions was not really a clash of religious faiths, since the anti-Buddhist faction did not recognize the Buddha as a religious entity different in kind from the indigenous *kami*. In other documents of the period, too, the

Buddha is referred to as "a *kami* from a neighboring land," "the *kami* of the Great T'ang [China]," and "the Buddha *kami* [*hotoke-gami*]."

In short, upon their introduction to the Japanese court, the Buddha and Buddhism became pawns in a struggle that was not religious but political, a struggle between the progressive Soga clan, which favored a broader international outlook for Japan, and the conservative Mononobe clan, which valued domestic traditions more highly. This is not to say that conflict between the two systems of belief on religious grounds was not possible, for they were indeed very different in many respects. Most notably, as already mentioned, Buddhism rejects and seeks to transcend the reality that Shintō affirms, a distinction displayed most prominently when we compare their views of the afterworld and of sin.

Pure Land Buddhism teaches that one way to seek release from the sufferings of this world is to strive for rebirth in a Pure Land, an ideal realm created by the merit of a buddha's long practice. Several such realms are described in Buddhist scriptures, but the most popular as an object of religious faith has always been that of the buddha Amida (Amitabha or Amitayus in Sanskrit), whose Pure Land is said to be far away to the west. Buddhist practitioners reborn in a Pure Land, relieved of the pains and distractions of the human realm, are free at last to devote themselves to the attainment of enlightenment, the ultimate Buddhist goal. Though doctrinally there were several interpretations of the Pure Land concept, in popular Buddhist faith it was generally regarded as a realm to which one went after death, distinct from the present world and attainable only through physical or religious transformation. The Pure Lands, described at length in Buddhist texts, are richly imagined realms, full of shimmering jewels, lotus ponds, golden pavilions, and religious symbols, but without the odor of human activity. The Buddhist hells, too, were a source of fascination to followers of the religion. Again, these realms were usually thought of as destinations after death, separate from the human realm.

The worldview of ancient Shintō was strikingly different. Its myths spoke of three worlds: Takamagahara (the Plain of High Heaven), Nakatsukuni (the Land Amid the Waters), and Yomino-kuni (the Land of the Yellow Spring). In *Kojiki den* Motoori Nori-naga remarked that the Plain of High Heaven "has mountains, rivers, plants, trees, grasses, and palaces, and all sorts of things and activities . . . just as this [human] realm does." In other words, business was conducted in heaven, as were the trades and sexual relations. The heavenly realm was envisioned as substantially the same as the human and contiguous with it, and the possibility of free travel between the two was affirmed. Yominokuni was the sub-terranean realm of the dead, a place of darkness, but it too was connected to the realm of the living (Nakatsukuni) and could be visited by living human beings, who could also return to the world. The realm of the dead was described as foul and dirty, but no further details were provided. Unlike the Buddhist Pure Lands and hells, the vision of ancient Shintō was predominantly worldly and lacked any idea of a transcendental realm.

The ancient Shintō concept of sin (*tsumi*, which also means of-fense, impurity) revealed a similar attitude. As Norinaga pointed out in *Ōbarae no kotoba goshaku* [Commentary on the Words of Great Purification], in ancient Japan *tsumi* was an all-embracing term, referring not only to evil behavior but also to physical afflictions, such as sickness and "feelings" of uncleanness (*kegare*). The pro-foundly self-critical, introspective concept of sin found in Bud-dhism was absent; in Shintō *tsumi* could be shaken off like dust or wiped away like a stain. In fact the same word, *harai*, was (and still is) used for Shintō exorcism and for shaking or beating off dust. Simplicity, directness, and purity of heart were the prime virtues, and this current has run beneath Japanese culture through the cen-turies. Eventually, as we will see, it came into conflict with the ethi-cal systems of Buddhism and Christianity.

Overt conflict between Buddhism and Shintō was avoided at the time of the introduction of the continental religion, to wait un-til the gradual unification of the Japanese state and the subsequent increase in national awareness led to a more developed conscious-ness of native traditions. At first the progressive Soga clan adopted

Buddhism in much the same spirit as other clans adopted their own clan *kami*. It was not until the reign of Emperor Temmu (r. 673–86) that the attention of the Japanese began to be drawn to the differences between Buddhism and Shintō. Until that time, people had gradually and unconsciously assimilated Buddhism into their lives and way of thinking. We can trace the first clear articulation of the difference between the two religions, and the first attempt to adapt Buddhism to Japan and Japan to Buddhism, to Prince Shōtoku (574–622).

The political conflict between the Soga and Mononobe clans eventually engulfed the imperial line, escalating to a bloody struggle for the throne between two factions of the imperial house. After a series of assassinations, the Sogas placed a woman of Soga lineage on the throne in 592. She reigned as Empress Suiko till 628. The year after her accession, Suiko appointed her nephew Prince Shōtoku regent. When he assumed control of the state, Japan was beset with difficulties. Dominion over the kingdom of Mimana, on the Korean Peninsula, had been wrested from Japan by Silla in 562, and some parties advocated its recapture and an attack on Silla. At home there was an increasing need to put an end to the power struggles among powerful clans and reinforce the imperial authority.

Stepping onto the stage of national affairs at this juncture, Prince Shōtoku sent an envoy to Silla, followed by an expeditionary force. He also established exchange with the Sui dynasty (581–618) in China. He is believed to have instituted the system of twelve court ranks, composed the Seventeen-Article Constitution (actually a declaration of general principles rather than a code of law), introduced the system of dating by imperial reigns and "eras," and directed the compilation of the historical chronicles *Tennōki* [Record of the Emperors] and *Kokki* [Record of the Nation].

The prince also urged the adoption of Buddhism as a means of raising the level of Japanese culture and providing the people with spiritual fulfillment. He studied the religion with the priest Eji from Koguryŏ and wrote commentaries on three pivotal sutras of Mahayana Buddhism: the Lotus Sutra, the Shrimala Sutra, and the

Vimalakirti Sutra. These commentaries are known jointly as the *Sangyō gisho* [Commentaries on the Three Sutras]. Buddhist concepts, along with those of the Confucian and Legalist philosophies of China, can also be found in the Seventeen-Article Constitution. Article 2, for example, reads in part: "Sincerely reverence the three treasures. The three treasures, viz. [the] Buddha, the Law, and the Monastic orders, are the final refuge of the four generated beings, and are the supreme objects of faith in all countries."[1]

Prince Shōtoku's understanding of Buddhism is best seen in the *Sangyō gisho*. While referring to pertinent Chinese commentaries, he felt sure enough of himself to effect a peculiarly Japanese interpretation of the sutras, even ignoring passages that could not be made compatible with the Japanese worldview. The chapter of the Lotus Sutra titled "A Happy Life," for example, includes the passage "Ever preferring meditation and seclusion, he cultivates and controls his mind."[2] The prince remarked that a person constantly practicing meditation in a secluded place would have no opportunity to spread the teachings of the sutra, and purposely twisted the passage to mean that one should keep one's distance from followers of Hinayana Buddhism, who devote themselves to meditation.

At this and other points where he deviated from the more orthodox interpretation of the text he remarked, "My interpretation is somewhat different" or "We do not follow this passage." The prince was clearly aware of both Buddhism's reality-denying, transcendental philosophy and his own reality-affirming, earthbound philosophy and tailored the former to suit the latter. The theme running through the *Sangyō gisho* is the identity of the sacred and the secular; there is a strong emphasis on the realization of ultimate truth in the midst of mundane existence. All positive activity in the everyday world is affirmed just as it is.

As an individual believer, however, Prince Shōtoku may have

1. Ryusaku Tsunoda, Wm. Theodore de Bary, and Donald Keene, eds., *Sources of Japanese Tradition*, vol. 1 (New York: Columbia University Press, 1958), p. 48.
2. Bunnō Katō et al., trans., *The Threefold Lotus Sutra: Innumerable Meanings, The Lotus Flower of the Wonderful Law, and Meditation on the Bodhisattva Universal Virtue* (Tokyo: John Weatherhill and Kōsei Publishing Co., 1975), pp. 222–23.

been more sympathetic to Buddhism's criticism of reality. The ancient piece of embroidered cloth known as the Pure Land Mandala is a depiction of the Pure Land in which the prince was believed to have been reborn; its sewing was overseen by his wife, Tachibana no Ōiratsume, after his death. Only fragments remain, but the mandala is thought to have included representations of one hundred tortoises. Four Chinese ideograms were stitched on the shell of each, and the resulting four-hundred-character text is believed to have been a memorial relating the origin of the mandala. The text of the memorial has been recorded in the *Jōgū Shō-toku hō'ōtei setsu*, a biography of Prince Shōtoku written in the late seventh or early eighth century. This work also contains the words, attributed to the prince, "The world is illusion; only the Buddha is truth." If these are in fact his words, they are extremely important, for they are the first evidence of the appearance in Japan of a way of thinking that is critical of this world.

The Japanese grasp of Buddhist teachings is further suggested by the inscription on the back of the mandorla of the Shakyamuni triad by the sculptor Tori Busshi in Hōryū-ji, dated 623. The inscription includes this prayer: "May [Prince Shōtoku, his mother, and his consort] rise to the Pure Land, with good speed rise to the Wonderful Reward [enlightenment]." This indicates that the Buddhist rejection of the world and its goal of transcendence had already begun to penetrate Japanese culture. The same, of course, would apply to the Pure Land depicted in the embroidered mandala, provided that the concept of the Pure Land was understood in the orthodox Buddhist sense.

During Prince Shōtoku's time Japan was actually ruled by a federation of clans; strong centralized imperial rule, the rise of a Japanese national consciousness, the awakening of the "Japanese spirit," and a clear recognition of the Buddhist worldview were all still to come. One of the most impressive characteristics of Prince Shōtoku is the way in which his writings and actions foretold the future. In Article 12 of the Seventeen-Article Constitution, for example, he called for the unification of the nation under the emperor: "In a country there are not two lords; the people have not two masters."[3] And in the *Sangyō gisho* he sought to adapt Buddhism to Japanese reality, while the inscriptions on the Pure Land Mandala and the Shakyamuni triad suggest that he had grasped the true essence of Buddhism. All this places him a giant step ahead of his contemporaries.

Though there are several early biographies of Prince Shōtoku, including the *Jōgū Shōtoku hō'ōtei setsu*, an account in the *Nihon shoki*, and the ninth-century *Jōgū Shōtoku taishi den buketsuki*, much of his life is shrouded in myth and hagiography, so that even today debate surrounds his actual words and deeds. For example, the *Jōgū Shōtoku hō'ōtei setsu* credits him with founding seven temples—Shitennō-ji, Hōryū-ji, Chūgū-ji, Hachioka-dera (also known as Kōryū-ji), Ikejiri-dera (also known as Hokki-ji), Tachibana-dera, and Katsuragi-dera—but this cannot be confirmed.

After the prince's death the Soga clan swiftly exterminated his family and gathered the reins of power into its own hands. But the Soga clan's domination was not to last long. From within the imperial house appeared a man of vision and force, Prince Naka no Ōe (626–71). He joined forces with the new intelligentsia of young men who had returned from studying in China and members of other clans who were disenchanted with the Soga regime and led them in revolt.

Prince Naka no Ōe's coup succeeded, and he proceeded to institute a strong centralized government with the emperor at its head, based on the model of T'ang-dynasty China (618–907). In 646, the year after the assassination of the Soga clan leader, Soga no Iruka, Prince Naka no Ōe issued a proclamation announcing reforms. These are known collectively as the Taika Reform, after the Taika era (645–50), and the system of government that evolved therefrom is often called the *ritsuryō* (criminal and civil statutes) system. The new centralized land and tax policies demanded a heavy sacrifice from the people, which eventually drove many peasants to abandon their fields and retreat to the mountains, but there was a pressing need at the time to strengthen the nation in response to a

3. Tsunoda, De Bary, and Keene, *Sources of Japanese Tradition*, vol. 1, p. 50.

perceived threat from China, and a certain degree of sacrifice was probably unavoidable.

For a while Prince Naka no Ōe remained one step removed from the throne, serving as regent. In 663 he lent military aid to Paekche in its campaign against the allied forces of Silla and China. When this venture met with defeat, he concentrated on domestic affairs. In 668 he was officially enthroned as Emperor Tenji and began to compile the Ōmi Code of laws. After a brief struggle to decide who would succeed Emperor Tenji upon his death in 671 (the Jinshin Disturbance), his brother Prince Ōama ascended the throne as Emperor Temmu (r. 673–86); he strengthened the *ritsu-ryō* system and compiled the Asuka Kiyomihara Code, which was promulgated in 689 by his widow and successor, Empress Jitō (r. 686–97). Thus was established a unified nation-state. Emperor Temmu's activities were not confined to politics. He played a pivotal role in the development of Japanese thought and culture, for with political unification and stability came a rise in national consciousness. At last the stage was set for the first real confrontation of Buddhism and Shintō.

Shintō enjoyed official support, while Buddhism was both supported and restricted by the government. The aspects of Buddhism that served the interests of the state and were compatible with traditional Japanese patterns of thought were encouraged. Those that did not fit this mold were restricted, ignored, or abandoned. This treatment did not kill Buddhism in Japan but did prune it, preparing the way for new, distinctively Japanese growth and for the eventual flowering of Japanese Buddhist thought and culture.

CHAPTER THREE

The Buddhist Adaptation

O NE OF THE FIRST HINTS of the gradual systematization of the Shintō pantheon into the present hierarchy, with the solar deity, Amaterasu Ōmikami, at its head, is found in a passage from ✓ the third volume of the *Shoku Nihongi* [Further Chronicles of Japan; 797] that notes that in the third year of the Keiun era (706) "tribute from Silla was offered to Ise Grand Shrine and other shrines of the seven provinces." This passage indicates that Ise Grand Shrine and the solar deity enshrined there were recognized as taking precedence over all other shrines and *kami* in Japan.

Amaterasu Ōmikami was originally called simply the sun deity (*hi no kami*). Gradually this deity was personalized and given the name Ōhirume no Muchi, meaning "the woman who worships the sun"; finally, during the reign of Emperor Temmu, she came to be known as Amaterasu Ōmikami, "Great Heaven-Illuminating Deity." At first she was worshiped as the progenitor of the imperial clan. As such she had no direct links to the other clans, but was simply one clan deity among many. As Emperor Temmu and his successors Empress Jitō and Emperor Mommu (r. 697–707) proceeded to strengthen the nation-state headed by the emperor, however, Amaterasu Ōmikami and her shrine at Ise came to occupy a place above all other deities and shrines.

With this, the hierarchy of Shintō deities began to take shape. Amaterasu stood at its apex, followed by the *kami* of the other clans directly related to the imperial clan, then the *kami* that had created the land of Japan, and finally the folk *kami* of the people. Rites and festivals dedicated to the *kami* were established and regulated in the Taihō Code (701), which included a Code of Shintō Worship (Jingiryō). This document represents the rise of Japanese national consciousness and is a quintessential expression of Japanese thought as it took form in the beliefs and practices of Shintō.

Meanwhile, Buddhism was meeting with a twofold reaction: official patronage on the one hand and strict government regulation on the other. The Clerical Code (Sōniryō) of 624 is an example of the latter. The Clerical Code, modeled on T'ang China's ordinances governing the Taoist and Buddhist clergy, strictly regulated the activities of the members of the Buddhist Order in Japan. It thus stood in clear contrast to the Code of Shintō Worship, which was designed not to restrict but to establish and encourage Shintō rites. Though the term *ryō* was used at this time to mean an administrative code, while *ritsu* usually referred to a penal code, the Clerical Code was strongly punitive; to each of its twenty-seven articles was appended the penalty for violating the article, ranging from disciplinary labor, such as cleaning temple halls or assisting in the repair of temple edifices, to revocation of clerical status. The latter penalty was especially harsh, since it meant the offender was subject to taxation, from which members of the Buddhist Order were exempt.

The government took steps to regulate the activities of the clergy because of corruption within the religious community. It is said that Empress Suiko decided to institute the so-called *sōgō* system of regulation when the case of a Buddhist priest who had murdered his father came to light in 624. The *sōgō* system, staffed by high-ranking government-appointed priests, was designed to oversee every aspect of the lives of the Buddhist clergy. Supervision of the clergy by the civil government cannot be ascribed entirely to the corruption of religious institutions and practitioners, however. Characteristically Japanese political motives and cultural patterns can also be detected, particularly in the Clerical Code.

Many of the government regulations contravened the codes of

morality and religious discipline of the Buddhist Order. For example, one of the most widely followed texts of Buddhist moral discipline in East Asia, the Sutra of the Perfect Net, urges the propagation of the Buddhist teachings among the masses and the construction of "places of practice"; Article 5 of the Clerical Code expressly forbids these activities. The Sutra of the Perfect Net forbids members of the clergy to associate or affiliate themselves with the nation's sovereign or high-ranking officials, yet Article 19 of the Clerical Code specifies the etiquette that priests must observe with government officials. In fact, the sutra expressly forbids the institution of civil codes regulating clerical activities.

The reason for forbidding the propagation of the Buddhist teachings among the masses was strictly political. The codes and laws enacted to build a centralized state required considerable sacrifice from the people, and the government wished to prevent popular dissatisfaction from crystallizing and growing into a mass movement. Thus any activity that rallied people in groups was feared. A famous priest of the period, Gyōki (668–749), was well known for his good works among the people, but he was censured in 717 for "inciting the masses" in violation of the Clerical Code. Perhaps the government had reason to fear; Gyōki is said to have gathered crowds of over a thousand. Interestingly, the government called on Gyōki's services, granting him the highest ecclesiastical rank (*daisōjō*), when it set about raising funds for the construction of the Great Buddha of Tōdai-ji, a huge bronze sculpture. The cooperation of the entire nation was required for this massive project, and the government needed Gyōki's ability to mobilize the populace.

What is most striking about the subjugation of the Buddhist clergy by the government is that the struggle never grew into an ideological contest. The contrast between the Clerical Code and the Code of Shintō Worship shows that the government made a conscious distinction between its treatment of Buddhism and of Shintō and recognized that certain elements of Buddhism were not to its liking. But this recognition never hardened into an ideological stance or elicited a strong intellectual response or organized resistance from the Buddhist establishment. The regulation of the Buddhist religion, and even rejection of parts of it, was resolved within the context of the tacit cultural assumptions shared by Japanese both inside and outside the Buddhist Order.

The same attitude can be seen in regard to the government's adoption of "three sutras for protecting the nation." The three sutras chosen—the Golden Light Sutra, the Sutra on the Benevolent King, and the Lotus Sutra—all contain passages that declare the preeminence of the Buddhist Law over secular law, yet Japanese government leaders did not respond to this challenge on an ideological level. Instead, they endorsed the passages that could be exploited for their purposes and ignored those that could not. In the same way, Emperor Shōmu (r. 724–49) made use of the Sutra of the Perfect Net, which describes the "lotus-womb world" ruled over by the buddha Vairocana, as a symbolic model for his own reign, invoking the parallel in his plan to construct the Great Buddha of Tōdai-ji. Though the same sutra contains passages that clearly deny the state's authority to regulate the clergy, the emperor did not perceive these as having any pertinence. Nor, in fact, did Japanese priests. They certainly were intellectually aware of the Buddhist rejection of reality and its supramundane claims, but their awareness failed to give birth to any resistance to secular rule.

The Chinese clergy reacted differently. In China, whether priests enjoyed a status above secular authority or were required to pay homage to the emperor was the subject of vigorous debate. The priests insisted that, on the authority of such texts as the Sutra on the Benevolent King, they were above the authority of the ruler and resisted attempts to regulate them. The government, for its part, attacked the status of the priests and the authority of the scriptures they relied on. In fact, it has been suggested that the Sutra of the Perfect Net and the Sutra on the Benevolent King were composed by Chinese priests in the fifth century to support their bid for autonomy. In Japan no such debate arose, at least at that time. Only with the advent of Saichō (767–822), the founder of the Tendai sect of Buddhism, did opposition to government regulation of the clergy become an issue.

The difference between the Chinese and Japanese reactions was due partly to the length of Buddhism's history in the two nations and the degree to which it had penetrated the national consciousness, but the nature of the two states must also be considered. China, an amalgam of peoples, was subjected to successive invasions, and its central government was overthrown periodically. In response, a highly developed philosophy of government legitimizing political authority was developed. Underlying the Chinese stress on orthodoxy and legitimate political authority was the basic insecurity and instability of imperial rule in the Middle Kingdom, which allowed the possibility of opposition to and criticism of the regime. Japan, meanwhile, being an island nation, was less vulnerable to invasion; therefore imperial rule was neither articulated nor attacked ideologically. Whatever struggles for the throne there were, and there were many, the authority of the throne itself was preserved, and opposition to this authority found little opportunity to ripen into action. Even centuries later, when warrior clans ruled Japan, they were careful to preserve the illusion of governing in the emperor's name. That is why the Japanese imperial line has survived down to the present.

Though the Buddhist scriptures taught the superiority of the clergy to lay authority, Japanese Buddhists, with few exceptions, did not press or, often, even recognize the point. The Japanese cultural traits noted earlier were evident in both the regulation and the selective encouragement of Buddhism. These traits shaped the way in which Japanese culture assimilated and adapted Buddhism, which then flowered in a distinctively Japanese fashion.

An outstanding example of the patronage that was extended to Buddhism at this time is the great increase in the construction of temples. According to contemporary records, in 624, during the reign of Empress Suiko, there were 46 temples in Japan. By 692, during the reign of Empress Jitō, their number had grown to 545. In less than seventy years the number of temples had increased more than tenfold. Even allowing for some exaggeration in the figures, the rapid increase is striking. What was the reason for this sudden interest in constructing Buddhist temples, and what purpose did it serve?

Most of the temples were built to ensure the buddhas' and bodhisattvas' protection of the nation, a belief widely accepted at the time. Temples built for personal reasons were usually clan temples (*uji-dera*) dedicated to the peace and prosperity of the clan and were linked closely with the veneration of clan ancestors, replacing the old clan tombs in function. We have seen that such tombs first appeared toward the end of the Kofun period as small mounds with side entrances, designed to house the dead of the clans that began to form at that time. Gradually the larger and wealthier clans began to construct magnificent large-scale tombs as symbols of the clans' prosperity and power. This tendency was condemned in the Taika Reform, which, partly to check the power of the clans, decreed less grandiose burial places. The introduction of the Buddhist custom of cremation around that time also contributed to the decline of ostentatious tombs. The energy formerly invested in building tombs was transferred to constructing clan temples, which became the new symbols of the glory of the clan and the expression of hopes for its future peace and prosperity. Likewise, Buddhist images were enshrined in these temples to ensure their protection of the clan.

The magical power ascribed to Buddhist images in this early period becomes evident when we examine the layout of structures within temple precincts. Four temples are frequently cited as representing the evolution of temple precincts up to the mid-eighth century. They are, in chronological order, Asuka-dera, Shitennō-ji, Hōryū-ji, and Yakushi-ji. By studying the changes in temple layout we learn that at the earliest stage the pagoda, which was supposed to enshrine relics of the Buddha, was centrally placed. Gradually, however, the *kondō* (image hall) replaced it in the center of the temple grounds. Relics were originally given the central location for the magical powers they were believed to have. As Buddhist sculpture became more sophisticated, images were allotted the space

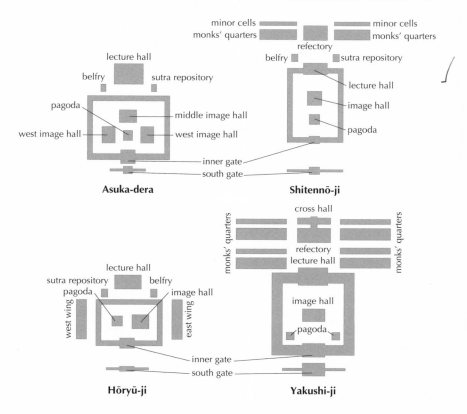

The Changes in Temple Layout

once held by relics, a sign that images were believed to fulfill the same magical function. The *kōdō* (lecture hall), where the scriptures were read, studied, and taught, was a later addition.

The same evolutionary process can be observed in China, but in India just the opposite occurred: there, the monks' quarters were the first to develop, followed after the Buddha's death by a stupa or *caitya* (sanctuary) housing relics of the Buddha, and finally, when the art of Buddhist sculpture developed, an image hall. Early Buddhist images in India were not regarded as being imbued with magical powers but were sculpted in the desire to be once again, if only symbolically, in the presence of the Enlightened One.

The layout of temple precincts provides one clue to the way in which the Japanese assimilated Buddhism. Another clue is found in the popularity of ceremonial recitations of the "three sutras for protecting the nation" in hope of such secular benefits as the peace of the nation and security and ease in the present life. At about this time Buddhist services dedicated to the ancestors of the imperial line were instituted, and the practice spread to include private observances of the anniversaries of the deaths of parents, spouses, children, and other kin. In China there were ten Buddhist observances after death (seven observances until the forty-ninth day of death, one observance on the hundredth day, one after a full year, and one after three years), but in Japan the number of observances continued to grow over the centuries, eventually including ceremonies on the seventh, thirteenth, fiftieth, and even hundredth anniversary of death. This trend indicates how strongly Buddhism in Japan was associated with ancestor veneration and is further testimony to the distinctively Japanese perception of the religion.

When the capital was moved from Fujiwara-kyō to nearby Nara (then known as Heijō-kyō) in 710, the fourth year of the reign of Empress Gemmei (r. 707–15), thus ushering in the Nara period (710–94), the major temples were moved, as well. During the reigns of Empress Genshō (r. 715–24), Emperor Shōmu (r. 724–49), and Empress Kōken (r. 749–58), temple construction flourished, and the seven great temples of Nara were built: Tōdai-ji, Kōfuku-ji (formerly Yamashina-dera), Gangō-ji (formerly Asuka-dera and Hōkō-ji), Daian-ji, Yakushi-ji, Saidai-ji, and Hōryū-ji. Moving the capital to Nara was part of the process of consolidating a strong, unified, centralized imperial government that had begun with the establishment of the *ritsuryō* system in the Taika Reform. Emperor Shōmu's creation of a network of regional temples for male and female clergy (*kokubun-ji* and *kokubunni-ji*, respectively) and his construction and dedication of the Great Buddha of Tōdai-ji were also linked to this broader political scheme.

In 741 the emperor decreed the founding of *kokubun-ji* and *kokubunni-ji* in all the provinces of Japan. The former were officially known as "temples to seek the protection of the nation from the four *deva* [heavenly] kings, housing the Golden Light Sutra" and the latter as "temples for the elimination of sins, housing the Lotus Sutra." Each temple housed ten copies of one of those two sutras plus a copy of the Golden Light Sutra written in gold in the emperor's own hand. There was a Chinese precedent for Shōmu's action, but the main motivation was probably to pray for the peace and prosperity of the nation in the face of the social unrest resulting from the increasingly heavy burdens caused by implementation of the *ritsuryō* system and the suffering caused by the natural disasters and epidemics that occurred with great frequency at that time. The *kokubun-ji* and *kokubunni-ji* contributed greatly to the development of regional culture, an unintended but beneficial by-product of imperial policy. In the ninth or tenth century these temples began to lose government protection, and most became defunct. The remains of many can still be seen throughout Japan today.

Tōdai-ji stood at the head of all these local temples. Its *kondō*, housing the Great Buddha, was the largest wooden structure in the world. Construction of the hall is thought to have begun around 749, the year the casting of the buddha image was completed, and was completed around 757. (The present structure dates from the early eighteenth century and is only two-thirds the size of the original.)

Emperor Shōmu proclaimed his intention to construct the Great Buddha in 743, and casting began in 747. The image represented Vairocana, a universal buddha who is a symbol of the unity of the cosmos. The Chinese rendering of the name Vairocana, usually transliterated into Japanese as Birushana or Rushana, means Universal Light or Light Illuminating All.

In the Sutra of the Perfect Net, one of several in which Vairocana appears, the universe is represented as a thousand-petaled lotus blossom, in the center of which he sits. On each of the petals of the lotus sits a Great Shakyamuni Buddha, the form in which Vairocana appears to sentient beings. Each petal contains ten billion worlds, and in each world is a Small Shakyamuni, an emanation of the Great Shakyamuni. The enormous scale of the

Buddhist worldview is indicated by this symbolic representation of universal harmony, but Emperor Shōmu utilized it more prosaically to represent the ideal image of his own government. It was with this in mind that he initiated the Great Buddha project. It is possible that the emperor was genuinely responsive to the universality proclaimed in the Buddhist teachings (he referred to himself as a "slave of the Three Treasures"), but it is extremely doubtful that he grasped the message of Buddhism as a world religion, transcending the boundaries of individual states.

The construction of the Great Buddha was undertaken as a prayer for the achievement of an ideal, unified nation-state, and it became a national project, demanding the wealth and labor of the entire country. By the time it was completed the resources of the provinces had been depleted. An entry in the *Shoku Nihongi* for the seventh month of 757 complains that "the people are made to suffer by the construction of Tōdai-ji, and the clans worry over their sufferings." As resistance to the continued expenditure of capital and labor rose, the government turned to the popular priest Gyōki and announced that the *kami* of Usa Hachiman Shrine (the main Hachiman shrine of Japan, located on Kyūshū) desired the successful completion of the statue—which was finally achieved under Empress Kōken in 749. Three years later the world's largest Buddha image was dedicated in a magnificent ceremony led by the Indian priest Bodhisena, who had arrived in Japan in 736.

The Buddhism of the Nara period is typified by the so-called six Nara schools: Sanron, Hossō, Jōjitsu, Kusha, Ritsu, and Kegon. *School* is a more appropriate term than *sect*, for these were branches of Buddhist scholasticism rather than different religious approaches to the faith. Most temples at the time were not affiliated with a particular school, but permitted the study of a variety of teachings, and individual priests frequently studied the doctrines of more than one school. The six schools together constituted, in effect, a curriculum of Buddhist scholarship.

The doctrines of the Sanron (three treatises) school were based on two treatises (*shastra* in Sanskrit) by the great Indian Buddhist philosopher Nagarjuna (ca. 150–ca. 250)—the Treatise on the

Middle (*Madhyamaka-shastra*) and the Treatise on the Twelve Gates (*Dvadashamukha-shastra*)—and one by his disciple Aryadeva, the Treatise in One Hundred Verses (*Shata-shastra*). Though the Chinese versions of these works are slightly different from what we know of the Sanskrit originals, they faithfully present the Mahayana teachings of Emptiness (*shunyata*) and the Middle Way.

The Sanron school, the first of the six Nara schools to be introduced to Japan, was transmitted by a priest from the Korean kingdom of Koguryŏ named Hyegwan, who arrived in Japan in 625. He had traveled to China to study these teachings with the founder of the school there, Chi-tsang, and upon his return to Koguryŏ was ordered by his king to take the teachings to Japan. His Japanese disciples Chizō and Dōji also traveled to China to study and again transmitted the teachings to Japan. (Their introductions of the teachings are called the second and third transmissions, respectively.) The Sanron school was quite active even before the Nara period, and Hōryū-ji was originally an academic center for this school, though in the Nara period the Hossō school was headquartered there.

The Jōjitsu school was based on the Treatise on the Completion of Truth (*Satyasiddhi-shastra; Jōjitsu ron* in Japanese), composed by Harivarman in the third century. This treatise explicated the concept of Emptiness in a Hinayana context, and was transmitted to Japan along with the teachings of the Sanron school.

The Hossō school expounded a Mahayana analysis of existence. Because it taught that the "storehouse consciousness" (*alayavijnana*) is the sole source of all existence, it was also called the Consciousness Only school. The first transmission of its teachings took place when the Japanese priest Dōshō (629–700) of Gangō-ji traveled to China to study the teachings under Hsüan-tsang, the illustrious Chinese master who had brought many Consciousness Only texts and teachings back from India and was in the process of translating them. (Dōshō asked to be cremated at his death, and this is said to be the origin of the custom in Japan, though there remains some disagreement on this point.) Many other priests followed in his footsteps and traveled to China to study the teachings.

The priests Chitsū and Chitatsu are credited with the second transmission of the Hossō school, and the priests Chihō, Chiran, and Chiyū with the third.

The Hossō school, blessed during the Nara period with a succession of brilliant scholar-priests, was in many ways the most outstanding school of Nara Buddhism. Giin (d. 728), a gifted disciple of Chihō, was much revered for his wisdom. He is said to have founded five temples, including Ryūgai-ji (also known as Oka-dera). His disciples included the well-known priests Gyōki, Gembō (d. 746), and Rōben (689–773). Gyōki, whom we have already discussed, was so highly esteemed for his wide travels teaching the common people and for his good works in their behalf—building bridges, digging reservoirs and wells, and constructing free rest stops for travelers—that he was popularly called "the bodhisattva Gyōki." Gembō traveled to China and, after returning to Kōfuku-ji, was credited with the fourth transmission of the Hossō school. He served as a government adviser, as well, eventually becoming embroiled in politics and being exiled to Dazaifu, on Kyūshū.

The Kusha school was based on the *Abhidharmakosha* (*Kusha ron* in Japanese) of Vasubandhu (fourth or fifth century), which analyzes the components of existence according to Hinayana Buddhism. It was transmitted to Japan along with the teachings of the Hossō school.

The Ritsu school was centered on the Buddhist precepts (*sila*) and monastic regulations (*vinaya; ritsu* in Japanese). In this school, which had its origins in China, observance of the *sila* and the *vinaya* was the focus of practice. A great teacher of the precepts was sought in China, with the result that the Chinese priest Chien-chen (pronounced Ganjin in Japanese; 688–763) finally arrived in Japan after six attempts, during which he lost his eyesight. When he reached Japan, in 753, he was sixty-five years of age. The year after his arrival an ordination platform was constructed at Tōdai-ji and some four hundred believers, including members of the imperial family, received the precepts. Ordination platforms were also built at Yakushi-ji, in Shimotsuke (present-day Tochigi Prefecture), and Kanzeon-ji, in Dazaifu. For the next several decades

all members of the clergy were ordained at one of those three platforms. In 759 Tōshōdai-ji, in Nara, was built as a residence for
Chien-chen, and there he lived and taught until his death. This
temple became the headquarters of the Ritsu school.

Chien-chen's disciples included both Chinese priests who had
gone to Japan with him and Japanese priests. His Chinese disciple
Ssu-t'uo (pronounced Shitaku in Japanese) wrote his biography,
on the basis of which his Japanese disciple Ōmi no Mifune (also
known as Mahito Genkai) in 779 composed *Tō dai wajō tōsei den*
[The Journey of the T'ang Great Master to the East], a moving account of the adventures of Chien-chen's party on its journey to
Japan.

The Flower Garland Sutra (*Avatamsaka-sutra; Kegon-kyō* in Japanese), the central scripture of the Kegon school, contains some of
the profoundest teachings of Mahayana Buddhism. This sutra ex-
plicates the great unity of the universe (in the form of Vairocana)
and the endless activity that unfolds and is sustained by that great
unity. The Chinese priest Tao-hsüan (pronounced Dōsen in Japanese; 702–60) transmitted Kegon texts to Japan. In 740 the Silla
priest known in Japan as Shinjō (d. 742) lectured the Hossō priest
Giin's disciple Rōben on the Flower Garland Sutra. Shinjō is recognized as the first master of the Kegon school in Japan, and
Rōben as the second. Rōben, who lived at a subtemple of Tōdai-ji,
devoted himself to the construction of the Great Buddha and was
known at the time as one of the Four Sages, together with Emperor
Shōmu, Gyōki, and the Indian priest Bodhisena. The teachings of
the Kegon school played an important role in the project, so much
so that Tōdai-ji also came to be known as Dai Kegon-ji, "the Great
Kegon Temple."

In addition to the texts and teachings of the six Nara schools,
those relating to sects of Japanese Buddhism that would develop
later, such as Tendai, Shingon, the Pure Land sects, and Zen, were
taken to Japan at this time. In fact, almost all Buddhist thought
and literature was introduced to Japan during the Nara period.
That some texts that are no longer extant were once in Japan is
evidenced by surviving catalogues. We might imagine that this

means that the Japanese clergy of the Nara period possessed a tremendous breadth and depth of Buddhist learning, but in fact Buddhism was little more than an academic study for scholar-priests secluded in monasteries. While these priests may have gained an intellectual understanding of the religion, they had not yet made the faith or its philosophy truly their own.

CHAPTER FOUR

The Japanese Response

THE MAJOR SOCIAL ROLE of the Nara Buddhist clergy was to offer prayers and hold grand ceremonies for the peace and prosperity of the nation. In return, the priests were awarded high status and special privileges by the nation's rulers. But Buddhist ideas were not completely confined to monasteries; they had begun to spread to lay society, as well.

As Buddhism developed in Japan, its teachings began to attract the attention of the educated classes, eventually shaping their view of life. In a way, Buddhism was more alive among the cultivated laity than in the dry and dusty studies of the scholar-priests. Because lay believers were free to pick and choose sympathetic elements in the teachings, they assimilated Buddhism in a distinctively Japanese way strongly colored by traditional beliefs and sentiments. Though a general picture of the way in which Buddhism was absorbed by Japanese culture is provided by the activities of the clergy and government regulation of the religion, a more vibrant and perhaps truer picture of the emerging Japanese Buddhist consciousness is revealed by the writings of the educated laity.

Verses on the theme of impermanence in the poetry anthology known as the *Man'yōshū* provide us with many examples. The *Man'yōshū* includes poems dating from the reign of Emperor Nintoku, in the fourth century, to 759. It contains about 4,500 Japanese-style poems (*waka*), of which 30 or so are on the theme of impermanence. The relative scarcity of poems on this theme suggests that the concept of impermanence had not yet been generally accepted in Japan. It is true that the Japanese did not apprehend the idea of the impermanence of human life as an intellectual doctrine. Rather, the Buddhist teaching of impermanence acted as a medium for the generation of a distinctively Japanese concept of impermanence. In other words, the Buddhist doctrine of impermanence was articulated in a Japanese context. This can be seen in many poems in the *Man'yōshū* that might not be classified as Buddhist in the narrow sense.

The following poem by the warrior and poet Ōtomo no Tabito (665–731) is representative:

> Now that I am brought to know
> The vanity of human life,
> Sadness bows me down
> Deeper than ever.[1]

This poem was written in reply to condolences that Tabito had received on the death of his wife, who had died in 728 while he was stationed in faraway Dazaifu, on Kyūshū. He returned to the capital, Nara, in 730 and, alone in his house, recalled his wife's presence in the following two poems:

> My house forsaken by my love,
> And so desolate—
> How much more it pains my heart
> Than did my travels, grass for pillow.

> Each time I see this plum-tree,
> Which my darling planted,
> My heart swells with sadness
> And tears fill my eyes.

1. All poems from the *Man'yōshū* except that on page 55 are from Nippon Gakujutsu Shinkōkai, trans., *The Manyōshū* (Tokyo: Iwanami Shoten, 1940; New York: Columbia University Press, 1965).

Yamanoue no Okura (660–733) sympathized with Tabito's grief for his wife and composed a poem in Chinese offering his condolences. Borrowing Buddhist terminology, Okura's poem lamented the impermanence of human life and spoke of abandoning this defiled land to be reborn in the Pure Land. But this poem seems to be little more than a formal, intellectual gesture. Okura's true feelings were more vibrantly expressed in the Japanese poems that follow the Chinese ode. One reads:

> The bead-tree's flowers my darling saw
> Will be scattered
> While my tears have not dried.

Speaking as Tabito, Okura lamented that the flowers of the bead tree that his wife used to gaze at would fall before his tears ceased. Tabito's son Yakamochi (718–85), in turn, took Okura's poem as a model when he mourned the death of his own wife:

> In the garden that my darling loved
> The flowers still bloom;
> And a long time has passed,
> Yet my tears are not dry.

Both Okura and Yakamochi composed other poems on the impermanence of human life. Okura's is prefaced "An elegy on the impermanence of human life" and opens with the lines "We are helpless before time / Which ever speeds away." It closes in a similar vein: "And, cling as I may to life, / I know no help!" Yakamochi's poem is prefaced "On the uncertainty of life" and concludes with the following lines:

> Looking at life's changes,
> Unseen as the passing wind,
> Ceaseless as the flowing water,
> I cannot stop my tears streaming
> Like floods on the rain-beaten ground.

These poems are full of grief and resignation at life's impermanence, though a difference in nuance from the Buddhist teaching of impermanence is apparent. In Buddhism, with the realization of the impermanence of life is born the effort to find release from impermanence. Transcendence of life is the message that Buddhism emphasizes. But the poems on the theme of impermanence in the *Man'yōshū* merely lament life's impermanence: "Sadness bows me down," "I cannot stop my tears streaming," "I know no help!" No progression to another level is indicated in these poems; they are characterized by a surrender to the feeling of sadness, a wallowing in the sense of the emptiness of life.

This emotion was not restricted to the poets whose work appears in the *Man'yōshū* but was expressed by poets of later times, as well, representing the most typical formulation of the feeling of impermanence among the Japanese. Or perhaps it is more accurate to say that this was the Japanese interpretation of impermanence. Some critics have suggested a distinction between the Buddhist concept of impermanence and the concept of impermanence as manifested in Japanese culture. They call the Buddhist concept the *realization* of impermanence, its Japanese version the *feeling* of impermanence, emphasizing the pathetic and aesthetic components of the latter. In short, the Japanese perceived impermanence as a pathetic feeling, an almost aesthetic appreciation of life's frailty and emptiness.

This impulse was to contribute to the creation of great works of literature and art in later times, literature that reflected the feeling of "the pathos of things" (*mono no aware*), such as the *Genji monogatari* [Tale of Genji], the great novel written by the court lady Murasaki Shikibu in the early eleventh century. In the eighteenth century Motoori Norinaga, a scholar of the Kokukagu (National Learning) movement, which sought an essential "Japaneseness," free of foreign influences, in Japanese literature and thought, identified *mono no aware* as the theme that runs throughout the novel and stated that this diverged from Buddhist teachings. Buddhism, according to Norinaga, is a strict spiritual discipline that urges us to observe the impermanence of the human condition in order to cut the bonds that bind us to that state and to free us from the limitations of humanity; in the *Genji monogatari*, however, tears are

THE JAPANESE RESPONSE 53

shed for life's evanescence, but beauty is sought in its pathos. This, said Norinaga, is *mono no aware*. Admittedly, it was Norinaga's intent to deny any Buddhist influence in the *Genji monogatari*, but even making allowances for his bias, his interpretation of the novel is acute.

The literature of recluses and semirecluses, men and women who had retired from the world, often entering the Buddhist priesthood, was an important genre in Japan that also shows a strong Buddhist influence in a distinctively Japanese form. These recluses seemed to wander, rootless, in the world, but they did not seek a realm beyond the human. They were in retirement not away from the world but within it.

Perhaps the best-known work in this genre is the collection of essays by Yoshida Kenkō (1283–1350) titled *Tsurezuregusa*. One of the most famous passages from these essays is on transience: "If man were never to fade away like the dews of Adashino, never to vanish like the smoke over Toribeyama, but lingered on forever in the world, how things would lose their power to move us! The most precious thing in life is its uncertainty."[2]

Zeami (1363–1443), the creator of the Noh dance-drama, wrote in a similar vein in his work on the aesthetics of Noh, *Fūshi kaden* [The Transmission of the flower]: "It is the withering of the flower [the ideal of the artist's expression] that is especially attractive." The twelfth-generation master of the Ikenobō school of flower arranging, Senkei (fl. mid-fifteenth century), left the oral teaching "Arrange together flowers from past and present, far and near," by which he meant that true beauty is to be found in the contrast of glory and decline, full bloom and fading flowers, and that the ideal should be sought by arranging together flowers from different seasons. This is said to be the highest ideal of the art of Japanese flower arranging; it was also the ideal of the warriors of the Age of the Warring Provinces (1467–1568), a time of constant strife among powerful regional lords, who found beauty in their lives

2. Donald Keene, trans., *Essays in Idleness: The* Tsurezuregusa *of Kenkō* (New York: Columbia University Press, 1967), p. 7.

precisely because they were always aware that death was imminent.

Appreciation of the beauty of the transience and fragility of human life and willingness to give oneself to this feeling could, on
occasion, take the form of rejection of the Buddhist teaching of
transmigration. Two poems composed by Ōtomo no Tabito to that
effect appear in the drinking poems of the *Man'yōshū*:

> If I could but be happy in this life,
> What should I care if in the next
> I became a bird or a worm!
>
> All living things die in the end:
> So long as I live here
> I want the cup of pleasure.

These poems, composed during the reign of Emperor Shōmu, at
the height of the glory of Nara Buddhism, indicate the way in which
the teachings of Buddhism were popularly understood at the time.

A slightly later work by the priest Keikai, *Nihon ryōiki* [Miracle
Stories of Japan; ca. 822], reveals how little the Buddhist ideas of
transmigration and rejection of this world had yet taken root.
Nihon ryōiki is the oldest extant Japanese collection of Buddhist tales,
a genre that was to play a large part in popularizing Buddhist teachings. Though this early work mentions the Buddhist Pure Land, it
is not depicted as a realm that transcends the present world.

When the Japanese first encountered the concept of withdrawal
from the world, they tended to ignore its more radical implica-
tions; when the ancient Japanese truly sought to withdraw from
the world of men and women, they retreated into the world of nature. Many of the poems in the *Man'yōshū* celebrate nature, and
quite often the events of human life are likened to natural events.
Love poems speak of the echoes of human passion in the cries of
birds and the trilling of insects, and the impermanence of the
changing seasons becomes a metaphor for the transience of human existence:

Nothing in the world endures:
Has the time come already
For the blossoms of the cherry tree
Here beside my hut to fall?

In the *Man'yōshū*, humanity and nature are perceived as one. This is one reason that the controversial Buddhist doctrine of enlightenment for plant life was easily accepted in Japan. This belief is frequently reflected in literature. For the Japanese, nature was a friend and plants had feelings. The appreciation of and emphasis on feeling is characteristic of the early Japanese attitude toward Buddhism and, as one of the major threads of Japanese culture, has continued to the present.

Some say that their reliance on feeling has prevented the Japanese from penetrating the deepest truths of Buddhism, but this is not necessarily so. Though there may be a difference between, for example, the Japanese perception of impermanence and the more specifically Buddhist teaching of impermanence, this does not mean that the truth has not been grasped, only that it has been grasped in a Japanese manner. Instead of expounding the truth of Buddhism in terms of rhetoric and logic, the Japanese preferred to express their understanding in the language of feeling.

Since earliest times the Japanese have been blessed with a high degree of artistic creativity, as the earthenware vessels and figures of the Jōmon period and the figurines of the Yayoi period testify. The supreme expression of Japanese artistry, however, is seen in Buddhist sculpture. Quite aside from their technical and artistic brilliance, these images' expressiveness and modeling embody the emotional language through which the Japanese grasped Buddhism's profoundest teachings.

Japanese art history divides early Buddhist sculpture into three periods: the Asuka period (538–645); the Hakuhō period, further divided into early (645–71) and late (672–710); and the Tempyō period, also divided into early (710–52) and late (753–94). There is a clear evolution in the style of Buddhist images over this 256-year span. Images of the Asuka period are more stylized than later works. Their modeling is flat and two dimensional, and their poses are static. Faces are childlike, and so are proportions; heads are unusually large. The bridge of the nose is flat and is joined to the brows. The eyes are almond shaped, the lines of both upper and lower lids gently curved. The robes of the images are stiff and end in elongated points.

In the gradual movement toward realism, the plump faces of the earlier period grow more elongated and mature. In the early Hakuhō period, the line of the lower eyelid straightens out, while the upper line retains its curve; in the later Hakuhō period, this is reversed. The general proportions of images move toward realism and maturity, and oversized heads are no longer seen. Images become three dimensional, and robes no longer project stiffly but drape sensuously and are modeled in a fashion that makes them appear almost transparent. In the late Hakuhō period a new dimension, movement, is added, exemplified by the torsion seen in the statue of the bodhisattva Kannon (Avalokiteshvara in Sanskrit) in Kakurin-ji, Hyōgo Prefecture, and the statues of two bodhisattvas in the *kondō* of Yakushi-ji, in Nara.

In the Tempyō period Buddhist images become still more sophisticated and realistic. At last they are truly mature in face and form. A balance has been achieved between the stasis of the Asuka period and the movement of late Hakuhō: Tempyō images combine repose and dynamism. The eyes grow narrower and their expression more mysterious and otherworldly—perhaps, in such late-Tempyō sculptures as the wooden images in the *kōdō* of Tōshōdai-ji, under the early influence of the art of esoteric Buddhism. The bridge of the nose is more pronounced and is separated from the brows, imparting a nobler, more refined expression. In contrast to the bright, childlike optimism conveyed by images of the early Hakuhō period, later images give the impression of being mature adults who have experienced life's sufferings. Forms are fuller, exhibiting a ripe beauty.

The increasing realism of Buddhist sculpture led to cultivation of the skills necessary for sculptural portraiture, which first ap-

peared in the late Tempyō period. Fine examples of religious por-
traits include the image of Chien-chen in Tōshōdai-ji, the image of
the priest Gyōshin (d. 752?) in Hōryū-ji, and the image of Giin in
Oka-dera. The first two are hollow dry lacquer, and the third, lacquer over a wooden core.

The direct impulse for the evolution of Buddhist images outlined above was changes in Chinese styles of Buddhist sculpture,
for most of the sculptors and supervisors of sculpture projects in
Japan were of Korean or Chinese origin. Japanese efforts did not
stop with mere copying, however. Over the course of time, Buddhist sculpture took on a specifically Japanese flavor, and works
superior to the original models were even created.

CHAPTER FIVE

Heian Buddhism: Saichō and Kūkai

JAPANESE BUDDHISM has experienced several crucial turning points in its long history. One of these was the founding of the Tendai and Shingon sects in the early ninth century. As already mentioned, Saichō founded the former. The Shingon sect was established by Kūkai (774–835), also known by his posthumous title, Kōbō Daishi. To appreciate fully the great impetus that the birth of these two sects gave to the development of Japanese Buddhism, we must look again at Nara Buddhism, from which they sprang.

The Japanese tendency to affirm life and this world colored the acceptance of Buddhism in the Nara period, when it was patronized by the court as a magical means to ensure benefits and prosperity for the nation and its people. Of course, serious practitioners of Buddhism also appeared in the Nara period, ordained men and women who devoted themselves to the strictest Buddhist practice and discipline. They practiced good works in accordance with the Buddhist principle of compassion, earnestly studied Buddhist teachings, strove to raise the level of learning in society at large, and in general made great contributions to Japanese culture through the channel of Buddhism.

Among their charitable practices was the founding of lodgings for religious practitioners (*kyōden-in*), hostels for the destitute and homeless (*hiden-in*), dispensaries (*seyaku-in*), and hospitals (*ryōbyō-in*). Tradition has it that Prince Shōtoku established these four types of facilities at Shitennō-ji. Kōmyō, the consort of Emperor Shōmu, and Empress Kōken are also said to have devoted themselves to the construction of such buildings. There was even a dispensary in the *kondō* of Tōdai-ji. A catalogue of "medicines donated to Vairo-cana Buddha" has been preserved in the ancient storehouse in Nara called the Shōsō-in, as have various medicinal herbs. Some priests practiced medicine. In fact Chien-chen is regarded as one of the fathers of Sino-Japanese medicine. Priests known as *kambyō zenji,* or "healing masters," cared for the sick. The Hossō priests Gembō and Dōkyō (d. 772) were well known for their nursing activities.

Gyōki is the classic example of a priest who gave himself to good works. While traveling through the land winning converts to the Buddhist faith, he supervised the building of bridges, the digging of reservoirs, the development of harbors and moorings, and the construction of free rest stops for travelers. Another benefactor was Hiromushi (730–99), the sister of the poet Wake no Kiyo-maro. She entered the Buddhist Order and, as the priest Hōkunni, urged clemency for those who had been involved in an uprising led by the courtier Fujiwara no Nakamaro (also known as Emi no Oshikatsu; 706–64). Her pleas reduced their sentences of death to exile. She also extended her care to children who had been orphaned in famines. Many other acts of compassion have been recorded in the histories and biographies of the period.

As already noted, Buddhist temples were the centers of learning of the Nara period. Hōryū-ji, for example, was popularly known as Hōryū Gakumon-ji (Hōryū Temple of Learning). These religious institutions stimulated the birth of other institutions of learning: the Nikyō-in (Institute of Two Studies) of the scholar-official Kibi no Makibi (693–775) and the Untei-in library of the poet and courtier Isonokami no Yakatsugu (729–81) are two well-known examples. The "two studies" offered at the Nikyō-in were Buddhist and non-Buddhist learning. The Untei-in, the first public library in Japan, had halls for meditation and debate. The contributions of Nara Buddhism to literature and art were also substantial. With

Buddhist patronage and inspiration, great masterpieces of architecture, sculpture, and painting were created.

Nevertheless, the activities of the clergy were not always above reproach. Their main occupation was to offer prayers and services for the protection of the nation and the health of the sovereign. With this role came the rewards of rank and power, and some priests exploited these in a way most unsuited to their vocation. Gembō and Dōkyō, for example, participated actively in government, became involved in factional infighting, and lost sight of their true duties as members of the clergy.

Emperor Kōnin (r. 770–81) attempted to reform the government and the clergy by issuing a series of laws and imperial edicts. His successor, Emperor Kammu (r. 781–806), moved the capital from Nara first to Nagaoka and then, in 794, to Heian-kyō (later called Kyoto), thus ushering in the Heian period (794–1185). He took unprecedentedly strict measures against the Nara temples. When the capital had been moved to Nara in 710, the temples had relocated with the court, but Emperor Kammu made certain the Nara temples were left behind upon the move to the new capital. The seriousness with which he regarded the situation can be seen in the fact that from 783 to 805 he issued more than thirty edicts restricting the power and activities of Buddhist institutions.

Emperor Kammu also extended greater patronage than ever to Buddhism, but always in a form that was antagonistic to the vested interests of the Buddhist institutions of Nara. He founded many new temples in and around Kyoto, including Bonshaku-ji, in Ōmi, and, in 796, Tō-ji and Sai-ji, in Kyoto, ostensibly to protect the capital but also to compete with the Nara temples. He encouraged and supported Saichō and Kūkai, who founded sects that eventually robbed the Nara temples of most of their power and influence.

Saichō was born in Sakamoto, in Ōmi Province (present Shiga Prefecture) in 767. At the age of eleven he became a disciple of the priest Gyōhyō (722–97), who was living at the local *kokubun-ji*. Two years later the boy took the tonsure, abandoned his lay name, Hirono, and adopted the religious name Saichō. He received the precepts at the age of eighteen at the ordination platform of Tōdai-ji, thus officially becoming a priest. But only three months later he retired to Mount Hiei, northwest of Kyoto, and remained there in solitary practice, living in a hermit's hut, for thirteen years.

Saichō's reason for retreating from the world is given in the biography written by his disciple Ninchū: "Lamenting the transience of human life and the decline of the Buddha's law, he retreated to the mountains." Saichō himself recorded his motives in the five vows he wrote immediately after going to Mount Hiei: "The three realms [of desire, form, and formlessness] are filled with suffering, and nowhere is there peace. How pitiful are all living things. All is sadness, and nowhere is happiness to be found. Life is like a breeze, which cannot be stayed; our bodies are like dew, which soon disappears." He confessed his own folly with the words "most foolish of fools among fools, maddest of madmen among the mad, this ignorant living being, the lowly Saichō." The first vow proclaimed that he was making the vows for the sake of "the unsurpassed, supreme truth."

Saichō retired to Mount Hiei in 785, the year after Emperor Kammu had moved the capital to Nagaoka. He had witnessed the zenith of Nara Buddhism, with its emphasis on the academic study of Buddhism on the one hand and its heavy involvement in secular affairs and the world of politics on the other. This experience had undoubtedly led him to seek the ultimate truth of the Buddhist religion and to search for a unified teaching transcending the doctrines of the Nara schools. Retreating to Mount Hiei gave him the opportunity to pursue these goals.

The conclusion Saichō reached during his intensive and solitary search was that the truth of a single, unified, supreme Buddhist teaching was to be found in the doctrine of the One Vehicle (*ekayana* in Sanskrit) expounded in the Lotus Sutra. At the age of twenty-one, three years after secluding himself on Mount Hiei, he built there the Ichijō Shikan-in (Hall for Meditation on the One Vehicle), now the Kompon Chūdō (Central Hall) of Enryaku-ji. After ten more years of study and practice, he began to lecture on the Lotus Sutra and the teachings of the Chinese T'ien-t'ai (Tendai in Japanese) sect, which took that scripture as its central inspiration.

Saichō decided to travel to China to further his studies. Having been granted permission by the emperor, he set sail in 804. His ship was turned back by violent winds and deflected to Kyūshū, but he embarked again in the seventh month and arrived in China about two months later. He spent a little over eight months there studying the T'ien-t'ai teachings, as well as those of esoteric Buddhism, the precepts and monastic regulations, and meditation practices. In 806, the year after his return, he received permission to establish the Tendai Lotus sect on Mount Hiei. This alarmed the Nara schools, and they responded with protests and disputation of Saichō's doctrinal authority for making such a move.

The priest Tokuitsu of the Hossō school represented the Nara Buddhist establishment in attacking Saichō's teachings. In response, Saichō wrote *Shō gonjitsu kyō* [The Mirror Illuminating the Provisional and Ultimate Teachings] in 817, *Shugo kokkai shō* [Essay on the Protection of the Nation] in 818, and *Hokke shūku* [Superior Verses on the Lotus Sutra] in 821. Tokuitsu supported the distinctions of this world, asserting that the teaching of the "three vehicles" was ultimate and that the One Vehicle was a provisional teaching. (The three vehicles were those of *shravakas*, or "hearers," and *pratyekabuddhas*, or the self-enlightened, both of whom seek personal enlightenment; and bodhisattvas, who seek the enlightenment of others as well as personal enlightenment.) Saichō defended an all-embracing, unifying point of view, insisting that the teaching of three separate vehicles to salvation was merely a provisional, expedient means (*upaya* in Sanskrit) and that ultimate truth, represented by the One Vehicle, lacked such distinctions. Each of the debaters was accurately representing the teaching of his own form of Buddhism: the Hossō school insisted on the reality of the three vehicles as firmly as the Tendai sect affirmed the ultimate truth of the One Vehicle.

Saichō devoted all his energy to establishing the Tendai sect, in whose teachings he had found the ultimate truths of human life, all existence, and religious practice. A major obstacle was the fact that the Tendai sect lacked an ordination platform of its own and had to rely on one under the control of the Nara schools. Though Saichō's disciples might study and take the tonsure on Mount Hiei, they were not officially priests until they had received ordination in Nara; and once in Nara for that ceremony, it was inevitable that some of the followers of the new Tendai sect would be drawn to the glory of Nara Buddhism and fail to return to Mount Hiei.

Saichō resolved to build his own ordination platform on Mount Hiei and to institute an ordination ceremony that was based not on the Hinayana precepts and monastic regulations that were in use in Nara but on a Mahayana system of precepts and regulations. Strangely enough, though most of the doctrines studied in Nara were Mahayana, the daily life of the priests was based on the Hinayana precepts, as was the ordination ceremony. Saichō, in moving to abandon the Hinayana discipline and institute a Mahayana system in its place, made Buddhist history: as a result, for the first time doctrine and practice in Japan would be unified in a system true to the essence of Mahayana.

As the first step, in the fifth month of 818 Saichō drew up a six-item description of the training that his disciples on Mount Hiei would receive according to the Mahayana precepts and presented it to the court. Three months later he added eight minor regulations, and in the third month of the next year he presented a four-item document to the court describing the differences between Hinayana and Mahayana temples and their regulations and urging the establishment of a One Vehicle temple governed by the Mahayana precepts.

Of course the Nara schools protested vehemently, and the government refused his request to establish a Mahayana ordination platform on Mount Hiei. Though the government was critical of the Nara schools, the existence of an ordination platform and the *sōgō* office in Nara facilitated government control of Buddhism. The authorities feared that permitting an ordination platform on Mount Hiei would make it harder to control the clergy. In 820 Saichō presented to the court a work titled *Kenkai ron* [Treatise on

Manifesting the Precepts], in which he cited the teaching, in the Sutra on the Benevolent King, that it was wrong for a nation's ruler to attempt to govern the Buddhist Order and requested reconsideration of his proposal.

Permission for a Mahayana ordination platform was not forthcoming during Saichō's lifetime, however. In the fourth month of 822 he fell ill. Knowing that he would soon die, he gathered his disciples and delivered his last wishes: "Do not carve images for me, do not copy sutras for my sake. Only carry out my wishes. . . . Within the aspiration to enlightenment there is food and clothing, but within food and clothing there is not the aspiration to enlightenment." He died in the sixth month of the year, at the age of fifty-five. Through the good offices of those who had been close to him, permission to establish his Mahayana ordination platform was finally received from the court seven days after his death. On the twenty-sixth day of the second month of the following year, the court allowed the founding of Enryaku-ji, on Mount Hiei. The ordination platform was actually completed six years after Saichō's death.

Saichō's establishment of the Tendai sect is important in the history of Japanese Buddhism for three reasons. First, it signified the independence of Buddhism from secular authority. Second, it was the first sect to grow out of an individual's religious faith and ideals. And third, it marked the first appearance in Japan of an all-embracing form of Buddhism that strove for the highest ideals. Saichō's preaching against the *sōgō* system is the clearest example of the first point. In support of the second point we have his statement, in his petition for permission to travel to China, that he depended "on the sutras, not the treatises." The treatises were objects of philosophical analysis and debate, while the sutras were objects of faith. And in support of the third point we may note that it was precisely because the One Vehicle teaching of the Lotus Sutra embraced the most sophisticated of Mahayana teachings—Tendai, Kegon, esoteric Buddhism, Zen—that Mount Hiei continued to be the greatest center of Japanese thought, both Buddhist and non-Buddhist, for centuries.

Saichō's younger contemporary Kūkai is so widely known in Japan that the very term "Great Master"—Daishi—almost always brings him to mind. Many legends about him persist, and much of his life is veiled in mystery. Kūkai was born in the district of Tado, Sanuki Province, on the island of Shikoku. At the age of fourteen he traveled to the capital with a maternal uncle, under whom he studied the Chinese classics. He entered the imperial college at seventeen and studied Chinese philosophy. This did not satisfy him, however, and he turned to Buddhism.

Leaving the college, he returned to Shikoku, where he made a pilgrimage to its sacred mountains. At the age of nineteen he took the tonsure at Makiosan-ji, in Izumi Province (now part of Osaka Prefecture). He composed the *Sangō shiiki* [Guide to the Three Teachings] in 797, when he was twenty-three (some sources say he prepared a first draft at the age of seventeen), in which he compared the merits of the teachings of Confucius, Lao-tzu, and Shakyamuni. Confucianism, he concluded, is "the petty breeze of the vulgar world," Taoism "the sleight of hand of hermit-sages." Buddhism is superior to both.

Kūkai's activities from that time until his departure for China almost ten years later are unclear, but he probably pursued his studies at the Buddhist institutions of Nara. He was sent to China on the first ship of the official party that departed in the seventh month of 804, when he was thirty. By coincidence, Saichō was on the second ship, but the time was not yet ripe for the two masters to meet. The day after the four ships of the party set sail from Taura, in Hizen Province (present Nagasaki Prefecture), a gale scattered the travelers. Two months later only two ships arrived separately in China—the first carrying Kūkai, and the second bearing Saichō. The third had been struck by another gale and driven ashore on an island to the south, and the whereabouts of the fourth were never to be known, happenings that confirm how hazardous travel between Japan and China was, as Chien-chen's six attempts to reach Japan had demonstrated earlier.

Kūkai's party landed in Fu-chou in the tenth month of 804. In the twelfth month he headed for the capital, Ch'ang-an. Visiting the city's major temples, he met Hui-kuo (746–805) of the temple Ch'ing-lung-ssu and was entrusted with the teachings of the Chen-yen (Shingon in Japanese) sect of esoteric Buddhism. Chen-yen means "true words," and refers to the practice of reciting sacred formulas known as mantras. The esoteric Buddhism of China aimed to unite individuals and the Buddha in voice, body, and mind through the threefold practice of mantras, *mudras* (ritual hand gestures), and mandalas (sacred drawings symbolizing the cosmos and the Way to enlightenment). It had only recently been introduced to China from India and Tibet.

The historic meeting between Kūkai and Hui-kuo probably took place in the sixth month of 805, the last year of Hui-kuo's life. Originally Kūkai had planned to study in China for twenty years, but he felt that his goal had been accomplished once he had acquired the Chen-yen transmission from Hui-kuo, and he changed his plans, leaving Ch'ang-an in the third month of the following year and arriving at Dazaifu, Kyūshū, in the tenth month, after about two years in China.

Kūkai remained on Kyūshū for nearly a year, then moved to Makiosan-ji, where he had taken Buddhist orders. Only in the seventh month of 809 did he proceed to Kyoto, after receiving government permission, to take up residence at Takaosan-ji (also known as Jingo-ji), near the capital. It was at this point that the relationship between Kūkai and Saichō began.

On the twenty-fourth day of the eighth month Saichō sent one of his disciples to Kūkai with a request to borrow a certain esoteric text. Thus began a correspondence between the two masters. Saichō was forty-two and Kūkai thirty-five. Kūkai later moved for a while to Otokuni-dera, also near Kyoto, and while he was there Saichō visited him in the ninth month of 812. In the eleventh and twelfth months of that year Saichō and almost two hundred other priests, including Saichō's disciples, received the esoteric transmission at Takaosan-ji. Saichō had also studied the esoteric teachings while he was in China, but not, he felt, in sufficient depth, and for this reason he tried to learn as much from Kūkai as he could, sending his disciples to the younger master to borrow scriptures.

At first Kūkai complied with Saichō's requests, but when Saichō asked to borrow a commentary on the esoteric Sutra of the Principle of Wisdom, Kūkai refused. He insisted, in perfect agreement with the teachings of esoteric Buddhism, that the secret treasury of teachings could only be transmitted directly, from teacher's mind to disciple's mind. That was the first sign of strain in the relationship. It came to an end when Saichō's leading disciple, Taihan (b. 778), who had been studying with Kūkai, did not return to his master despite Saichō's earnest pleading. In the fifth month of 816 Kūkai dictated for Taihan a letter to Saichō in which Taihan severed all ties with his former master, putting an end at the same time to relations between Saichō and himself.

A month later Kūkai petitioned the court for permission to establish a monastic center on Mount Kōya (near present Nagoya), where he had roamed as a youth. When official sanction was received, he began the necessary preparations, and around the eleventh month of 818 he began construction of Kongōbu-ji there. Early in 823 he was entrusted with Tō-ji, in Kyoto, as a center for esoteric Buddhist practice, and its name was changed to Kyō'ō Gokoku-ji. That temple became the base of Kūkai's activities, including the performance of esoteric ceremonies at the request of the court. Next to this temple, in the twelfth month of 828, he established the Shugei Shuchi-in, an educational institution open to the common people. *Shugei shuchi* means "bestow a general education," and thus this institution resembled a modern university. Out of consideration for the children of the less privileged, tuition was free.

Kūkai wrote *Himitsu mandara jūjūshin ron* [Treatise on the Secret Mandala of the Ten Stages of the Mind], and a summary of it titled *Hizō hōyaku* [The Jewel-Key to the Secret Storehouse], in 830. *Himitsu mandara jūjūshin ron* categorized various philosophical systems, both Buddhist and non-Buddhist, in ten levels, crowned by the esoteric teachings of Shingon. The work is both a masterly thesis in comparative religion and a comprehensive system of thought. Through the Shingon teachings, Kūkai aimed to reveal and explain the mystical realm that exists within and motivates the universe.

He was the first to articulate the doctrines of Shingon Buddhism in organized form, in such works as *Ben kemmitsu nikyō ron* [Treatise on the Exoteric and Esoteric Teachings], *Sokushin jōbutsu gi* [The Meaning of Becoming a Buddha in This Body], *Shōji jissō gi* [The True Meaning of the Voiced Syllable], and *Unji gi* [The Meaning of *Hum*]. No one can compare with Kūkai in his simultaneous achievement of profound mystical religious experience and creation of a systematic religious philosophy.

Kūkai's health was weakened by an intractable carbuncle in 831, and he retired to Mount Kōya in the summer of the following year. He died on the twenty-first day of the third month of 835, at the age of sixty-one.

A comparison of Saichō and Kūkai is in many ways a study in contrasts. Saichō was closely associated with Emperor Kammu, whereas Kūkai was close to Emperor Saga (r. 809–23). The differences in political trends during those two reigns were partly responsible for the differences in the attitudes of the two Buddhist leaders. Of course Emperor Saga respected the wishes of his predecessor and continued to support Saichō, but he leaned more strongly toward Kūkai. Kūkai, unlike Saichō, demonstrated a cultivated, cosmopolitan sensibility. He was, for example, highly gifted in the art of calligraphy and, along with Emperor Saga and the courtier Tachibana no Hayanari, was considered one of the three great calligraphers of the time.

Though both Kūkai and Saichō eventually established their headquarters on mountains far from the court, Kūkai had studied in the great Chinese capital of Ch'ang-an, at that time perhaps the most advanced city in the world, learning about the urban Buddhism of Ch'ang-an and China's government-sponsored temple system. When he returned to Japan, he secured the support of the Heian court but also remained on good terms with the old guard of Nara Buddhism.

Kūkai studied the newest sect of Chinese Buddhism, which the Chinese court was actively patronizing. Saichō, on the other hand, studied a sect that had originated almost three centuries earlier and had long been in decline in China, only recently having experienced a revival. Saichō had the obstinacy of the rustic about him—he was not the sophisticate that Kūkai was. That aspect of Saichō's character can be seen in his determined opposition to the Nara Buddhist establishment.

Kūkai entered China as a "resident foreign student" and stayed there about two years. Saichō was a "visiting student" scheduled to return to Japan after only one year, though he actually stayed in China a little more than eight months. The range of what he learned was, perforce, limited. Perhaps, given these disparities in their lives and characters, the personal differences that arose between them over the esoteric teachings were inevitable.

Although Saichō and Kūkai were very different in many ways, both contributed to the creation of Japan's most sophisticated system of thought. Saichō illuminated the ultimate truth of the cosmos; Kūkai exposed its innermost secrets. The result was a great universal philosophy that encompassed and synthesized all currents of thought at that time, Buddhist and non-Buddhist. For Saichō, the ultimate truth was to be found in the Lotus Sutra's teaching of the One Vehicle of the Law. Kūkai's ultimate truth was the secret inner core of mystery represented by the teachings of esoteric Buddhism, on the basis of which he constructed a great philosophical and intellectual system.

One more distinction between Saichō and Kūkai was to play a very important part in the fortunes of the Buddhist sects founded after their deaths. Kūkai brought the philosophical basis of the Shingon sect to completion and left little doctrinal territory unexplored. For that reason, after his death the sect concentrated on cultivating the mystical religious experience that lay at the core of Shingon doctrine, placing greater emphasis on practice than theory. Mount Kōya became a holy place where the secret teachings were passed from master to disciple and mystical experiences were sought. The trend toward an overemphasis on mystical practice and the relative lack of emphasis on doctrine led to the sect's eventual degeneration into a system of magical practices—though of course we must not forget that an expansive and profound doctrinal structure underlay these practices.

Saichō, on the other hand, left room for further philosophical development of the Tendai sect. His mountain monastery evolved into a great center of intellectual activity after his death, as a series of eminent Tendai thinkers prepared the way for the culmination of Japanese Buddhist thought—the doctrine of original enlightenment, discussed in the next chapter. Mount Hiei also produced the founders of the major sects of Buddhism that developed in the Kamakura period (1185–1336). Tendai placed considerable emphasis on practice, eagerly incorporating esoteric teachings, but its priests devoted their greatest efforts to doctrinal studies, and Mount Hiei came to be regarded as the authoritative source of truth in matters of Buddhist philosophy.

CHAPTER SIX

Tendai Philosophy:
The Ideal and the Real

TENDAI PHILOSOPHY reached its pinnacle in the absolute monism represented by the doctrine of original enlightenment. Saichō himself was greatly influenced by the most sophisticated developments of Mahayana thought, represented by such scriptures as the Lotus Sutra and the Flower Garland Sutra and the practices taught in esoteric and Ch'an (Zen) Buddhism. Esoteric doctrines were enthusiastically incorporated into the Tendai system by his disciples Ennin (794–864), Enchin (814–91), and Annen (841?–901?). The absolute monism of the doctrine of original enlightenment was then developed by Ryōgen (912–85), Genshin (942–1017), Kakuun (953–1007), and other thinkers from the late Heian to the mid-Kamakura period.

In the Lotus Sutra and the Flower Garland Sutra, sentient existence is divided into ten realms, or states. The human state is midway between the highest state, that of the Buddha, and the lowest, that of hell. We are drawn equally to good and evil and can move either way, like the needle of a gauge. In fact, all aspects of human existence are dual: good and evil, birth and death, self and others, youth and age, male and female, husband and wife, parents and children, mind and body, beauty and ugliness, wealth and poverty, high and low estate, pleasure and pain. Yet these dichotomies are characteristics only of provisional reality, temporary divisions of what is originally one. The Treatise on the Awakening of Faith in the Mahayana, one of the main canonical sources of the doctrine of original enlightenment, teaches that true enlightenment (original enlightenment) lies in the realm of nonduality, of Emptiness (*shunyata*), which transcends the dichotomy of enlightenment and nonenlightenment. To search for enlightenment in contrast to nonenlightenment is to cause confusion.

This philosophy applies to an absolute being (God or the Buddha) or an absolute realm (nirvana or the Pure Land), as well. The truly absolute being, the truly absolute realm, can be discovered only by breaking through the dualistic conceptions of human beings versus God, ordinary beings versus the Buddha, or the Saha-world (this world) and the Pure Land, and realizing the nondualistic identity of the Buddha and ordinary beings, the fact that the Saha-world is precisely the Pure Land. In Pure Land Buddhism, for example, it is taught that Amida's Pure Land lies far away to the west; but it is mistaken to conceive of it as separate from our own realm of existence.

Genshin wrote, in *Kanjin ryakuyō shū* [The Essentials of Contemplation of the Mind; 1017]: "Just as my body is Amida and Amida is my body, the Saha-world is [the Pure Land of] Perfect Bliss, and [the Pure Land of] Perfect Bliss is the Saha-world." In another work attributed to him, *Mampō jinjin saichō busshin hōyō* [The Essence of the Buddha's Profound, Peerless Law], the same doctrine is explained at greater length: "Since cause and effect are both empty [*shunya*], how can the Pure Land be located in a specific place? The sutra says, 'Because of delusion there is the fortress of the three realms of existence [the realms of desire, form, and formlessness]; because of enlightenment, the ten directions are all emptiness. Originally there is neither east nor west. Where can we find north and south? . . . The nature of the mind is the *tathagata* [buddha] of original being. The ten directions are the unconditioned buddha-land. How is it possible to limit the buddha-land to one in the west?'"

To state that the body, the mind, and the Saha-world are nondual, are essentially identical, is to say that the Buddha and the Pure Land can be apprehended in the body, the mind, and this world. As *Kanjin ryakuyō shū* states: "When we turn a deluded thought into a thought on the principle of the true nature of things, we see the buddha-body in our own minds, the Pure Land in our own minds." The priest Kakuban (1095–1143), who founded the Shingi subsect of Shingon, restated this position as follows in his *Ichigo taiyō himitsu shū* [The Secrets of Essentials]: "Where is that [Pure Land of] Perfect Bliss? It fills all space. . . . When we realize this, we are no longer in the Saha-world but are immediately re-born in [the Pure Land of] Perfect Bliss. My body enters the body of Amida, and without any further transformation is immediately Dainichi [Mahavairocana]. My body comes forth from Dainichi, and this is the wonderful realization of buddhahood in this body."

The theory of nondual identity described above reveals eternity by transcending the concept of time. We tend to consider eternity the endless continuation of time, but that is not true eternity. No matter how far we extend time, as long as we treat it as measur-able we remain within its bounds. Only when we have transcended the concept of time—whether it be the short period known as a day or the endless period called eternity (that is, only when the present and the future are realized as nondual)—can we appre-hend eternity in the present moment. ~~Makura no sōshi [The Pillow Book]~~, the classic exposition of the Tendai doctrine of original en-lightenment attributed to Genshin, states this principle as follows: "Eternity and the present moment are one." "There is no distinc-tion between the beginning, the middle, and the end. How can we discuss eternity and today?" "The very first instant of thought is the eternally abiding, ever-unchanging thought. . . . Just as on the great ocean the waves of yesterday and the waves of today are one in substance, the thoughts of the three worlds [of past, present, and future] are only one thought." This is the doctrine of the eter-nal present, the eternity of the absolute moment.

When we apply this reasoning to birth and death (*samsara* in San-skrit), we see that people contrast death with life, and wish to negate death and prolong life. We seek immortality. But truly eternal life cannot be apprehended in this way. Only when we have aban-doned the concepts of both life and death, only when we have transcended the dichotomy of life and death—that is, only in the realm of neither life nor death, the realm where life and death are one—can we grasp eternity. If we negate, we must negate both life and death; if we affirm, we must affirm both. Only thus is true eternity to be found; only in this way can the fear of death be vanquished, and life and death accepted. *Shōji kakuyō shō* [Enlightenment of Life and Death], also called *Hommu shōji ron* [Treatise on the Original Nonexistence of Life and Death], attributed to Saichō, states: "The two facts of life and death are the wonderful activity of the one mind. The two paths of being and nonbeing are the true virtue of original enlightenment. . . . Thus the time when birth comes never comes, nor does the time when death leaves ever leave. . . . This is the wonderful coming of no coming, the true birth of no birth, the perfect leaving of no leaving, the great death of no death. Life and death are of one substance, and emptiness and being are nondual."

The Tendai doctrine of original enlightenment reveals the ultimate nature of existence, the ultimate realm, and elucidates its logical structure. The realm is that of nondual unity, and its logical structure is absolute monism. We must note, however, that even though the ultimate nature of existence is nondual unity, this does not mean that we can ignore the dualistic nature of ordinary existence. If we were to depict the human realm pictorially, we might represent it as a frame of dualism suspended in space (space representing nondualism, or emptiness). Emptiness is the essence of the human realm, while the frame is characteristic of ordinary existence. Human existence is twofold, comprising an ultimate, monistic aspect and an actual, dualistic aspect. To be born human entails the task of realizing the ultimate, monistic aspect within the actual, dualistic aspect. This is the purpose of human life.

It is a mistake to become attached to dualistic actuality and remain unaware of the monistic essence; but it is also wrong to abandon dualistic actuality and attach oneself to the monistic essence. The nondual must be vividly realized in the dual, and the dual must become actual because of the nondual. In Buddhism this is described as "not two but two" and "two but not two." The two great mandalas of the Shingon sect, the Diamond Realm mandala and the Womb Realm mandala, are graphic representations of these two principles.

Since the Buddha and ordinary human beings are one in essence, it is tempting to affirm the present state of ordinary human beings as identical to the state of the Buddha. This ignores, however, the dual nature of provisional reality. It is impossible to establish the activity of the nondual within the realm of duality. Only with the premise of the provisional reality of a dual nature does the nondual essence come alive. To interpret the doctrines of the identity of the Buddha and ordinary human beings and the nonduality of good and evil as an excuse to ignore the actual realities of the Buddha versus ordinary human beings, good versus evil—to declare that suffering sentient beings are, *as they are,* buddhas, that evil is, *as it is,* good—is the greatest folly and error. To rid oneself of delusion, it is important to see things as they are. In our world there are buddhas and ordinary people, good and evil, birth and death. Life is not eternal. This world is the Saha-world, and the Pure Land is far away. This is the teaching of relativistic dualism that is necessary for understanding our world.

The Tendai doctrine of original enlightenment is a radical absolute monism that supplies a logical framework for the idea that the ultimate nature of existence is nondual unity. It is a teaching that crowns the history of Buddhist thought and is one of the highest achievements in the history of philosophy. In Japan, it played a great role in Shintō, in philosophy, and in literature. But the Tendai priests tended to become too attached to the realm of the nondual essence and neglected to apply that principle to the dualistic human realm. When they did direct their attention to the dualistic realm of actuality, they were apt to affirm it *as it was* as the nondual essence and to teach that evil is good and ordinary people are buddhas. This encouraged people to indulge their desires and contributed to moral degeneration.

It was in reaction to the excesses arising from this warped interpretation of the doctrine of original enlightenment that Pure Land Buddhism emerged in the late Heian period and that Shinran,

Nichiren, Dōgen, and other Buddhist reformers appeared in the Kamakura period. The Pure Land teachings established a religious philosophy of relativistic dualism, focusing directly on the dualistic realm of actuality and opposing ordinary people to the Buddha, the Saha-world to the Pure Land. Kamakura Buddhism, in contrast, while firmly grounded in the dualism of the actual world, strove to activate the nondual unity within it.

Despite its eventual corruption, however, the Tendai doctrine of original enlightenment played an important part in the history of Japanese Buddhist thought. Without an understanding of it, the developments in late Heian and Kamakura Buddhism are unintelligible.

CHAPTER SEVEN

Pure Land Buddhism

THE LOFTY TENDAI DOCTRINE of original enlightenment was never meant to be divorced from the reality of the empirical world. Tendai philosophy incorporated two truths, the ultimate and the provisional, that were inseparable. But the scholar-priests of the sect, perhaps because in their mountaintop monasteries they were too isolated from the exigencies of secular life, failed to give full weight to the world of the provisional. As a result, the doctrine of original enlightenment became a convenient pretext, in the hands of degenerate priests and advocates of hedonism, for indulgence in the pleasures and temptations of the world.

In response, some Buddhists became critical of the doctrine; others were disenchanted because of historical circumstances as the long peace of the Heian period began to disintegrate. New dualistic teachings were drawn from the discredited monism of the doctrine of original enlightenment and gained strong support. Most representative of these dualistic systems was Pure Land Buddhism, which emphasized the aspiration for rebirth in the Pure Land of Amida.

Pure Land Buddhism originated in India but underwent further development in China and was introduced to Japan at an early date. Pure Land beliefs were part of Nara Buddhism and were incorporated into both Tendai and Shingon in the Heian period. Ennin, who inherited the leadership of the Tendai sect after Saichō's death, had studied the Pure Land teachings at the temple Chu-lin-ssu, on Mount Wu-t'ai, during his sojourn in China. He returned to Japan in 848, and the following year he established on Mount Hiei a center for *nembutsu* practice—contemplation and invocation of Amida, the central practice of Pure Land Buddhism—called Jōgyō Zammai-dō (Hall for Walking Meditation). He also instructed that the *nembutsu* mantra "Namu Amida Butsu" (I take refuge in Amida Buddha) be chanted without interruption for seven days after his death. It was in Ennin's time that Pure Land teachings and *nembutsu* practice began to flourish on Mount Hiei.

In the decades that followed, the Mount Hiei monastery complex fell on evil times. It was razed by fire twice, in 935 and 966. When Ryōgen became grand abbot, he worked to restore the sect's fortunes, and Mount Hiei once more became a renowned center of Buddhist activity. Ryōgen put special energy into the development of Tendai doctrine. His disciples included many fine scholar-priests, and the Pure Land teachings received considerable attention. Ryōgen himself wrote a work titled *Gokuraku jōdo kuhon ōjō gi* [On the Nine Types of Rebirth in the Pure Land of Perfect Bliss], and his disciple Genshin was the author of the famous *Ōjō yōshū* [Essentials of Rebirth].

Begun in the eleventh month of 984 and completed in the fourth month of the following year, *Ōjō yōshū* was three fascicles in length, divided into ten chapters. This work had a great influence not only on Pure Land teachings but also on Japanese culture in general and literature in particular. It was even introduced to China, where it enjoyed some popularity. The first part of the work explains the various types of delusions that afflict human beings, quoting scriptural sources to demonstrate that existence is impure, entails suffering, and is impermanent, and also describes in vivid detail the realm of hell, where those who commit egregious evil are reborn. In later ages, Genshin's descriptions of hell inspired the horrifying scenes in the paintings of hell known as *jigoku hensō zu*.

Genshin's intent was to describe the realm of delusion—and hell in particular—in such a way as to inspire dread of the karmic retribution for evil deeds. He aimed to awaken people to the impermanence and ignorance of the human state and then to teach them of the Pure Land so that they would abandon their attachment to this realm and seek a higher one. Genshin's description of the Pure Land was designed to inculcate the desire for rebirth there. To make the prospect even more attractive, he taught that Amida and his retinue of bodhisattvas would come to welcome believers and escort them on their way. Scenes of this welcoming (*raigō*) became a favorite subject of painting, along with gorgeous depictions of the Pure Land.

The latter part of *Ōjō yōshū* discusses the practices necessary for rebirth in the Pure Land, in particular the *nembutsu*, which Genshin regarded as the high road to the Pure Land because it was accessible to anyone and thus was a so-called easy practice. He considered *nembutsu* practice especially suited to the weak and the sinful.

Several other works on the *nembutsu* were written by Mount Hiei priests, including Kakuun, another disciple of Ryōgen. Pure Land *nembutsu* practice was incorporated into Shingon teachings, as well. Kakuban touched on the *nembutsu* in his *Ichigo taiyō himitsu shū* and *Amida hishaku* [Secret Interpretation of Amida]. Kakuban's conception of the Pure Land, however, derived from the absolute monism to which he subscribed, as did the Tendai interpretation at that time. Genshin's *Ōjō yōshū* recognized the dualistic aspect of Pure Land teachings, but the absolute monism of Tendai philosophy remained clearly visible in the background. For a Pure Land *nembutsu* doctrine with a strongly dualistic flavor, we must turn to the Buddhism of the Nara schools.

Pure Land teachings were incorporated in the Sanron school. The priest Yōkan (also known as Eikan; 1033–1111) wrote two works on Pure Land philosophy, *Ōjō jūin* [Ten Causes of Rebirth in the Pure Land] and *Ōjō kō shiki* [Rituals for Pure Land Assemblies]. Yōkan emphasized vocal *nembutsu*, the recitation of Amida's name, rather than mental conceptualization of that buddha, which was the Tendai and Shingon interpretation of the term *nembutsu*— appropriately enough, since *nembutsu* means "contemplating the Buddha." He taught that true concentration on Amida was achieved through vocalization and recommended that all other practices be abandoned in favor of the practice of chanting the formula "Namu Amida Butsu." Another Sanron priest, Chinkai (1092–1152), also proclaimed in his works *Bodaishin shū* [A Collection of Passages on the Aspiration to Enlightenment] and *Ketsujō ōjō shū* [A Collection of Passages Assuring Rebirth] that vocal *nembutsu* was "the truest of true practices."

Close examination of the writings of both Yōkan and Chinkai, however, reveals that they also held that human beings and the Buddha were essentially one on the ultimate level of truth. In *Ōjō jūin* Yōkan wrote: "The Buddha and human beings are identical in substance, without any difference." "Defilements and enlightenment are identical." "The cycle of birth and death is nirvana." "The nature of the mind is one; delusion and enlightenment are not two." "This mind is the Buddha." The same teachings are found in Genshin's *Ōjō yōshū*. Chinkai, in *Ketsujō ōjō shū*, taught that aspiration to enlightenment, which must be aroused through the practitioner's own efforts, is the true cause (*shōin*) of rebirth in the Pure Land: "Aspire to enlightenment and be reborn in [the Pure Land of] Perfect Bliss."

The first Japanese Buddhist leader to formulate a version of Pure Land teachings based on a truly dualistic approach was the founder of the Jōdo (Pure Land) sect, Hōnen (also known as Genkū; 1133–1212). In the limitations of the human state he perceived the impermanence and frailty of life and the deep human attachment to evil. He taught that human effort, which he called "self-power" (*jiriki*), was useless, and that instead one must depend upon the "other-power" (*tariki*) of Amida, by reciting the *nembutsu*, to attain rebirth in the Pure Land.

Before turning our attention to Hōnen's Pure Land teachings, however, let us look at the kind of Pure Land faith popular among the common people. Kūya (also known as Kōshō; 903–72) was a priest who propagated the *nembutsu* among the laity. Maintaining that "the marketplace is a place of practice," he would stand at bustling crossroads chanting the *nembutsu* and preaching to the masses, earning for himself such sobriquets as "the Holy Man [*hijiri*] of the Marketplace" and "the Holy Man of Amida." Carrying a staff topped by a deer's antler and striking a gong as he chanted, he wandered through the land urging people to adopt the *nembutsu* practice and performing charitable works, such as building bridges, digging wells, constructing roads, and burying abandoned corpses. The *nembutsu* first reverberated from the throats of the common people because of Kūya's labors.

Ryōnin (also known as Shō'ō Daishi; 1073–1132) also propagated the *nembutsu* among the people. In his youth he studied the Tendai and esoteric doctrines on Mount Hiei, but at the age of only twenty-two he retired to Ōhara, on the northern outskirts of Kyoto, where he built a residence and place of practice for himself that he called Raigō-in, after the welcoming of the *nembutsu* practitioner into the Pure Land by Amida and his bodhisattvas. There Ryōnin studied the Lotus Sutra and recited the *nembutsu*. When he was forty-five, he had a profound religious awakening. He perceived that the *nembutsu* he chanted contained the *nembutsu* of all other practitioners. This he called *yūzū nembutsu*, or mutually inclusive *nembutsu*. He began to preach this doctrine throughout Japan and built a center of *yūzū nembutsu* practice called Dainembutsu-ji at Hirano, in Settsu Province (present Hyōgo Prefecture).

Thanks to the efforts of such men as Kūya and Ryōnin, many lay people devoted themselves to the *nembutsu* practice in the hope of attaining rebirth in the Pure Land. Several collections of accounts of rebirth in the Pure Land (*ōjō den*) were compiled. The first was *Nihon ōjō gokuraku ki* [Japanese Accounts of Rebirth in the Pure Land], written in 984 by Yoshishige no Yasutane (ca. 931–1002), a priest on Mount Hiei. A little over a century later, the court official Ōe no Masafusa (1041–1111) wrote *Shoku honchō ōjō den* [Further Japanese Accounts of Rebirth in the Pure Land], and Miyoshi Tameyasu (1049–1139) wrote *Shūi ōjō den* [Gleanings of Accounts of Rebirth in the Pure Land] and *Go shūi ōjō den* [Further Gleanings of Accounts of Rebirth in the Pure Land]. The novice Renzen collected additional accounts in *Sange ōjō ki* [Accounts of Rebirth in the Pure Land Not Previously Recorded; 1139], and the aristocrat Fujiwara no Munetomo wrote *Honchō shinshū ōjō den*

[A New Edition of Biographies of Japanese Who Attained Rebirth in the Pure Land; 1151].

These stories of rebirth in the Pure Land include accounts of extreme practices. Self-immolation or drowning as a means to achieve rebirth probably did occur. But grotesque tales of cutting off a leg and fashioning a Buddhist image from the bone or peeling off the skin of a hand and painting a Buddhist image on it are hard to accept as fact. Regardless of our interpretation of these tales, however, they clearly attest to the presence of considerable numbers of fervent Pure Land believers.

Practitioners were divided into three types: *jikyōsha* (practitioners of the Lotus Sutra), *hijiri* (holy men), and *shami* (novices). *Jikyōsha* were believers whose main practice was devotion to the Lotus Sutra, but who also chanted the *nembutsu* in the hope of attaining rebirth in the Pure Land. The priest Chingen compiled a collection of accounts of *jikyōsha* titled *Dai Nihon hokke genki* [Accounts of the Practice of the Lotus Sutra in Japan; 1040–43).

Kūya was the exemplar of the *hijiri*. These practitioners retired to the mountains or roamed through the land reciting the *nembutsu,* sometimes propagating the teaching of the *nembutsu* practice as well. Those who traveled continuously and had no fixed abode were called "wandering *hijiri*"; others were known by the name of their place of retreat—for example, the *nembutsu* practitioners on Mount Kōya were known as "Kōya *hijiri*." *Jikyōsha* and *hijiri* included many priests who had been affiliated with temples but, lamenting the corruption of the Buddhist establishment as it became tainted with secular power, had left their temples to practice true Buddhism either in isolated mountain areas or among the common people.

Shami were lay believers who lived the same kind of life as ordinary people, eating meat, marrying, and working for a living, but devoted to the *nembutsu* all the same and working to teach those around them. Kyōshin (d. 866) is a classic example of this religious type. His story appears not only in accounts of rebirth in the Pure Land but also in Yōkan's *Ōjō jūin* and in the late-eleventh-century *Konjaku monogatari shū* [Tales of Times Now Past]. He is said to have built a hermitage in the province of Harima (present Hyōgo Prefecture). He married and fathered children, and made his living by working for someone in town. The only thing that distinguished him from his fellows was the remarkable fact that he never ceased to chant the name of Amida. The great Buddhist reformer Shinran (1173–1262) took Kyōshin as his religious ideal.

The accounts of rebirth in the Pure Land teach us that the most fervent faith in the Pure Land and the *nembutsu* was to be found among the common people. Of course, the faith described in these stories was not always "pure"—that is, it often combined a variety of practices and beliefs. For example, the *nembutsu* and the Lotus Sutra were often practiced together. The merits of faith were also sought through such practices as reciting and copying scriptures in addition to chanting the *nembutsu*. It was believed that the more one recited the *nembutsu,* the more merit one accrued, and the number of recitations was recorded by placing a bean in a basket for each recitation. This was called "quantity *nembutsu*" or "bean *nembutsu.*" The stories tell of hundreds of bushels of beans piled up in this manner. While such practices were magical and formalistic, the intensity of faith they indicate cannot be doubted; clearly a heartfelt wish for salvation underlay them.

As the Heian period drew to a close, the aristocratic culture began to disintegrate and the social order to collapse; the nation was beset with instability and disorder. The impermanence of life, and the folly and sinfulness of humanity, loomed large, and many people despaired, fearing that the period of the Decay of the Law (*mappō*) prophesied by the Buddha was at hand. As a result, the longing for rebirth in the Pure Land grew still stronger. It was this urgency that led, finally, to the development and propagation of a truly pure form of *nembutsu* belief and practice.

Let us briefly review the rise and fall of Heian culture. During the mid-Heian period, also known as the Fujiwara period (894–1086) because of the political dominance of the Fujiwara clan, the focus of Japanese high culture moved from the official realm to the private, from a Chinese-influenced culture to a Japanese-style culture. This development was effected by the aristocrats, who lived in great splendor. For years immense sacrifice, both financial and human, had been made to send missions to T'ang China to bring back Chinese culture. But in the late ninth century the T'ang dynasty began to decline, and missions to China ceased in 894. The T'ang dynasty fell in 907, and for a time there was no communication with the continent.

The development of a sophisticated aristocratic culture and the resurgence of indigenous traditions and sensibilities that emerged combined to forge an elegant, truly Japanese culture. The phonetic writing systems of *katakana* and *hiragana*, based on Chinese ideograms but better suited to writing in Japanese, were invented, and with them arose a new vernacular literature. Poetry anthologies, such as the *Kokin wakashū* [Collection of Japanese Poems Old and New], completed around 905, appeared, as well as prose narratives known as *monogatari*, such as the anonymous *Taketori monogatari* [Bamboo Cutter's Tale], *Ise monogatari* [Tales of Ise], *Yamato monogatari* [Tales of Yamato], *Utsubo monogatari* [Tales of Utsubo], and *Ochikubo monogatari* [Tales of Ochikubo]. Fiction writing reached a peak with Murasaki Shikibu's *Genji monogatari* around the turn of the eleventh century.

The literary genre of diaries (*nikki*) began with the *Tosa nikki* [Tosa Diary], written around 935 by the poet-aristocrat Ki no Tsurayuki, who adopted the persona of a woman in this work, since at that time literature in the vernacular was still regarded as a feminine province. This was followed by the *Kagerō nikki* [Kagerō Diary], by a woman known only as the mother of Fujiwara no Michitsuna, completed about 974, and the *Murasaki Shikibu nikki* [Diary of Murasaki Shikibu], completed about 1010. The court lady Sei Shōnagon's *Makura no sōshi* [Pillow Book], written around the turn of the eleventh century, marked the beginning of the genre of *zuihitsu*, or essays. In painting, *yamato-e*, or Japanese-style painting, developed and was used to decorate folding screens and sliding paper-and-wood partitions in the mansions of the aristocracy. *Yamato-e* was also used in illustrated scrolls, known as *e-maki*.

Buddhism was influenced by the rise of a truly Japanese culture, and at the same time supplied themes to literature and art. The

Japanization of Buddhism is perhaps seen most clearly in the Shintō-Buddhist syncretism known as *shimbutsu shūgō* (literally, "fusion of deities and buddhas"). Examples of this phenomenon can be found in the Nara period, when shrine temples (*jingū-ji*) were built in the precincts of major Shintō shrines, and sutras were enshrined and priests ordained for the benefit of the *kami*. In the Heian period Buddhist scriptures were recited before the *kami*, and Hachiman and other *kami* were designated "great bodhisattvas." In the mid-Heian period the theory that the *kami* and buddhas were essentially one gained popularity, gradually evolving into the doctrine of *honji suijaku* (original prototype and local manifestation), which held that the *kami* were manifestations of buddhas, bodhisattvas, and Buddhist deities. The title *gongen*, "provisional manifestation," began to be attached to the names of many Shintō deities, and temple shrines—the opposite of the Nara-period shrine temples—were constructed in the grounds of major temples, where a *kami* protecting the temple was worshiped. These *kami* and their shrines were called *chinju*, or pacifier and protector.

The development of the *honji suijaku* doctrine stimulated the emergence of such syncretic schools of Shintō as Sannō Ichijitsu Shintō, which incorporated Tendai doctrines, and Ryōbu Shūgō Shintō, which incorporated those of Shingon. The movement toward the synthesis of *kami* and buddhas also influenced literature, art, and architecture.

Unfortunately, dark clouds hung over the aristocratic culture of the Heian period even at the height of its splendor. This can be felt in the *Genji monogatari*. Though the novel depicts the full glory of Fujiwara culture under the great statesman Fujiwara no Michinaga (966–1027), who controlled the court, it is permeated by a strong sense of the transience of human life and the inescapability of the bonds of karma, lending the work a somber tone. The leading Fujiwara aristocrats became followers of Pure Land Buddhism, and several of them built temples designed to rival the Pure Land in splendor. Mototsune (836–91) built Gokuraku-ji, Tadahira (880–949) built Hōshō-ji, Kaneie (929–90) built Hōkō-in, Michinaga built Hōjō-ji, and Yorimichi (992–1074) built Byōdō-in at Uji, near the capital. Architecturally, these temples were modeled on the aristocratic residential style, and in design and decoration they represented the culmination of Heian art. The Hō'ō-dō (Phoenix Hall; also called the Amida-dō, or Amida Hall) of Byōdō-in, in particular, is a masterpiece—a gallery of the finest Japanese artistic achievement in its paintings and sculptures and the colorful decoration of its ceilings and pillars. So inspiring was it that a children's song of the time, recorded in *Go shūi ōjō den*, urged, "If you doubt the existence of the Pure Land, make a pilgrimage to the great temple at Uji."

Michinaga retired to Hōjō-ji during his final illness, and it was there that he died. According to the eleventh-century *Eiga monogatari* [Tales of Splendor], a history of the Heian court, he had threads of five colors tied between his hands and those of the statue of Amida there to ensure that he would be reborn in the Pure Land. Belief in the "thread-pulling *tathagata*" (*ito-hiki nyorai*) seems to have been widespread at the time and appears in several biographies and other accounts. Actual threads are still extant in the painting *Amida Rising over the Mountains*, said to be by Genshin but probably dating from the Kamakura period, now in Konkai Kōmyō-ji, Kyoto. The Fujiwara aristocrats' belief in the Pure Land was, however, little more than an extension of their worldly desires. It did not lead to transcendence or denial of the world, which could only spring from despair over the human state.

The aristocratic culture of the Fujiwara reached its peak with Michinaga and began to decline after he passed from the scene. Struggles for power and factional strife increased, leading to social unrest and then social upheaval. In addition, a succession of natural disasters plagued the nation. The year 1052 was widely believed to mark the beginning of the period of the Decay of the Law.

Finally the regional warrior clans, which had heretofore served the aristocracy, donned the mantle of authority that their masters had let fall—but only after quarreling viciously among themselves for its possession. Japan was wracked by bloody civil strife, often between father and son, brother and brother, during the Hōgen Disturbance of 1156 and the Heiji Disturbance of 1159. The brief twenty-nine years between the Hōgen Disturbance and the final defeat of the Taira clan (also known as the Heike) in 1185 saw as much change and upheaval as the preceding several centuries. This period of fear and danger produced an intense search for release from the uncertainty and evil of the world in the bliss of the Pure Land.

CHAPTER EIGHT

The Founders of Kamakura Buddhism

SINCE THE HŌGEN DISTURBANCE, the world has been in a state of confusion and only evil things have occurred." These are the words of the Tendai grand abbot Jien (also known as Jichin; 1155–1225), recorded in what can be regarded as Japan's earliest history written from a philosophical viewpoint, *Gukan shō* [Notes on Foolish Views; 1220]. The Hōgen and Heiji disturbances resulted in the ascent of the warrior class—especially the Taira clan—to a position of central authority. But the Taira adopted the lifestyle of the Heian aristocracy it had displaced and soon followed the nobility into eclipse. With the defeat of the Taira at the hands of another warrior clan, the Minamoto (also known as the Genji), in 1185, the Heian period came to an end.

The opening lines of the anonymous *Heike monogatari* [Tale of the Heike] announce the end of the age thus: "The tolling of the bell at Gion echoes the impermanence of all things. The glory of the mighty fades like the flowers of the *sala* tree. The strong do not long reign; they are no more than the dream of a spring night. The brave are destroyed, scattered like dust before the wind." The writer Kamo no Chōmei (1156–1216) extended these sentiments to all humanity in his *Hōjōki* [An Account of My Hut; 1212], a classic of medieval literature: "The waters of the river flow onward and are never twice the same. The froth that floats on its surface disperses and then forms again. It does not stay for long. Men and their dwellings in this world are no different."

Yet a rebirth of Japanese culture was imminent. Minamoto no Yoritomo (1147–99), the head of the Minamoto clan, established a shogunate, a military government headed by a shōgun, in Kamakura, near present Tokyo, in 1185; this marked the beginning of the Kamakura period (1185–1336). After Yoritomo's death actual power passed to shogunal regents appointed from the Hōjō clan, to which Yoritomo's wife, Masako, belonged. But with Yoritomo's disappearance from the scene, the cloistered emperor Gotoba (r. 1183–98), who had been cautiously observing and manipulating events from Kyoto, began to plot to restore power to the imperial house. His efforts culminated in an armed uprising in 1221 called the Jōkyū Disturbance, from the name of the imperial-reign era in which it occurred. Gotoba's forces were defeated, however, and he and two other cloistered emperors were exiled. This decisively ended the supremacy of the ancient court and confirmed the rule of the warrior clans and the establishment of a new social order under their aegis.

If the last years of the Heian period were characterized by pessimism and despair, the years following the Jōkyū Disturbance exhibited a new energy as the warrior clans began to control and manage the world they had inherited. Jien, affiliated as he was with the aristocracy (he was a member of the Fujiwara clan), characterized the early thirteenth century as a lawless age, but in fact the opposite was true. A good example is the Jōei Code of the Hōjō regent Yasutoki, enacted in 1232—a model of government by law. Of course, no matter how highly principled Yasutoki may have been and how effective his rule, a new age is always accompanied by turmoil. The ways of the previous age cannot be discarded all at once, and the new power base is always threatened with splintering and internal friction. The Hōjō regency was no exception.

Other factors also contributed to the unsettled nature of the times. Once again the nation was afflicted with a series of natural disasters that caused considerable social dislocation; in addition,

Japan was faced with the unprecedented threat of foreign invasion when twice, in 1274 and 1281, Mongol fleets approached the coast. Yet these internal and external threats differed from the symptoms of decline that had been evident in the late Heian period. They were perceived as challenges to be overcome in the process of consolidating the nation, and that is how the Japanese of the Kamakura period responded to them. Instead of reacting with resignation and despair, people faced these challenges boldly and attempted to change the unpleasant aspects of the reality they confronted.

The two giant wooden *vajra* (diamond) warriors (*kongō rikishi*) flanking the south gate of Tōdai-ji are concrete representations of this new spirit. The largest wooden sculptures in Japan, these images by the great Kamakura-period sculptors Unkei (d. 1223) and his colleague Kaikei stand over eight meters tall. Their bodies are muscular, their poses dynamic. Their glittering gaze seems to look reality in the eye.

The three greatest Buddhist leaders of the Kamakura period were Shinran, Dōgen, and Nichiren. Each, in his thought and writings, came to grips with actuality. In that sense their thought represented an evolution from denial of the world to its affirmation—though their affirmation must not be confused with the complete affirmation based on the Tendai doctrine of original enlightenment. They adhered to the critique of empirical reality that was the backbone of Hōnen's Pure Land teachings; yet while he sought to abandon this world, they sought to transform it. Shinran, Dōgen, and Nichiren went beyond both the Tendai doctrine of original enlightenment and Hōnen's Pure Land teachings, both absolute monism and relative dualism, both denial and affirmation of empirical reality.

A definite philosophical development can be detected between Hōnen's teachings and those of Shinran, Dōgen, and Nichiren, and thus it is appropriate to distinguish two phases in Kamakura Buddhism. In the first phase should be placed two figures in addition to Hōnen: Nōnin and Eisai, both propagators of the Rinzai sect of Zen Buddhism.

Hōnen, the founder of the Jōdo sect, was born into a locally powerful warrior family in the province of Mimasaka (present Oka-yama Prefecture) in 1133. When he was only eight his father was killed in a midnight raid, and this family tragedy is said to have spurred him to enter the Buddhist Order. At the age of fourteen he went to Mount Hiei, where he studied the Tendai teachings. He proceeded to explore the entire Buddhist canon and even trav-eled to Nara to study at the temples of the old schools, earning the epithet "Wisest of All." When he was forty-two he read the seventh-century Chinese Pure Land master Shan-tao's *Kuan-ching-su* [Com-mentary on the Sutra of Meditation on Amitabha Buddha]. Struck by the words "With one mind concentrate on the name of Amida," he took the *nembutsu* as his sole practice. Later he spread the teach-ing of the *nembutsu* from his base at Yoshimizu, in the Higashi-yama district of Kyoto, gaining followers ranging from the highest ranks of the nobility and warriors down to the lowliest peasants.

Hōnen delivered a famous lecture on *nembutsu* and answered questions about its merits at Ōhara in 1186, when he was fifty-three. The so-called Ōhara Debate was a pivotal point in his teaching. He wrote *Senchaku hongan nembutsu shū* [The Choice of the *Nembutsu* of the Original Vow], his most important work and the one that firmly established the Jōdo sect, in 1198. His activities and his popularity, however, aroused the envy and wrath of Mount Hiei and the Nara schools, which appealed to the government to prohibit the *nembutsu* teaching. In 1206 two of his disciples, Jūren and Anraku, were executed for their part in a scandal involving some court ladies, and this provided an excuse for harsh measures against the *nembutsu* movement. Hōnen was exiled to Tosa Prov-ince (present Kōchi Prefecture), on the island of Shikoku, in the second month of 1207. His disciples, including Shinran, were also exiled to distant parts of Japan. In the twelfth month of the same year Hōnen was pardoned. After remaining in Settsu for almost four years, he finally returned to Kyoto in the eleventh month of 1211, taking up residence at Ōtani, in Higashiyama. There he died on the twenty-fifth day of the first month of the following year. Persecution of the *nembutsu* movement continued after his death, however.

Hōnen taught that Buddhist practice must be adapted to the capacities of practitioners and the nature of the times. He believed that he lived in the period of the Decay of the Law and that people's capacities were severely limited. He selected the practice of the *nembutsu* as the most appropriate method of enlightenment for people of his time and encouraged them to abandon all other practices, thus steering Kamakura Buddhism away from the eclectic approach of Heian Buddhism. His teaching marked the first appearance of an exclusive, either-or approach in a Japanese Buddhist sect, a salient characteristic of Kamakura Buddhism as a whole.

Hōnen's religious conviction was that in the period of the Decay of the Law, inferior in capability as people are, they stand no chance of attaining enlightenment (buddhahood) on their own. They have no alternative to relying on the power of Amida for rebirth in his Pure Land. The scriptures of Pure Land Buddhism emphasize rebirth in the Pure Land through total reliance on the saving power of Amida's vow to save all sentient beings (other-power). Hōnen identified this saving power with the exclusive practice of the *nembutsu* as the "easy practice" best suited to ordinary people in the period of the Decay of the Law.

Nōnin introduced the teachings of Ch'an (Zen) Buddhism to Japan. In 1189 he sent two of his disciples, Renchū and Shōben, to China to study Ch'an teachings—in particular those of the flourishing Yang-ch'i branch of the Lin-chi (Rinzai) sect, which was at the peak of its popularity. The Japanese priests received certification of their enlightenment from Cho-an Te-kuang, the Dharma heir of Ta-hui Tsung-kao. With this link to the legitimate tradition of Ch'an, Nōnin established his own Daruma (Dharma) sect (named after Bodhidharma, traditionally regarded as the transmitter of Ch'an from India to China) and propagated the teachings in Japan.

Nōnin's Zen differed from the meditation (*dhyana* in Sanskrit, transliterated as *ch'an* in Chinese and *zen* in Japanese) practices that had been introduced under the aegis of the Nara schools and the Tendai and Shingon sects. Its fundamental teachings were that there is a "separate transmission" of Buddhism, that is, a transmission outside the scriptures; that the truth is not conveyed in words alone; that the truth must be experienced directly; and that buddhahood is attained by seeing one's true nature (buddha-nature). These ideas were new to Japanese Buddhism, and for that reason Mount Hiei appealed to the government in 1194 to forbid the propagation of Nōnin's Zen.

Eisai (1141–1215) was born in the province of Bitchū (present Okayama Prefecture). After studying on Mount Hiei he went to China in 1168 and stayed on Mount T'ien-t'ai, whence he took many T'ien-t'ai texts back to Japan. He traveled to China once more, in 1187, but this time he studied the Huang-lung branch of Lin-chi Ch'an under Hsü-an Huai-ch'ang. He returned to Japan in 1191. Because of the novelty of the teachings he took back with him, Eisai too was persecuted. His response was to write a defense of Zen teachings in three fascicles, titled *Kōzen gokoku ron* [Propagating Zen to Protect the Nation], which he completed in 1198, the same year in which Hōnen wrote *Senchaku hongan nembutsu shū*.

Eisai then went to Kamakura, where he founded Jufuku-ji in 1200 under the patronage of Masako, Minamoto no Yoritomo's widow. Two years later he was given a gift of land in Kyoto by the second Kamakura shogun, Minamoto no Yoriie, where he built Kennin-ji, which he made a place of practice not only of the new Rinzai Zen teachings but of Tendai and Shingon Buddhism, as well. He died in 1215 at the age of seventy-four.

Nōnin's disciples studied under Dōgen, the founder of the Sōtō sect of Zen Buddhism, and Nōnin's line thus disappeared, but Eisai's prospered. For one thing, Eisai's Zen was practiced in combination with the Tendai and Shingon teachings; not coincidentally, its absolute monism had much in common with the Tendai doctrine of original enlightenment. Though Eisai was persecuted for a short while, in the mid-thirteenth century his teachings were incorporated into the Tendai fold, with the result that the doctrine of original enlightenment was further bolstered. In addition, a little later many brilliant Chinese Lin-chi priests began to travel to Japan, which enhanced the sect's popularity. Perhaps because the teachings of this sect fit the lifestyle of the warrior class, it received the warm support of the shogunate. It is interesting to note that in this first phase of Kamakura Buddhism, in addition to Hōnen's relative dualism, which sprang from the historical reality of the decline of the Heian period, Nōnin and Eisai imported once again from the continent Buddhist teachings of absolute monism, this *non-dualism* time in the form of Rinzai Zen.

The second phase of Kamakura Buddhism began with Hōnen's disciple Shinran, the founder of the Jōdo Shin (True Pure Land) sect. He was born in Kyoto in 1173 to Hino Arinori, a minor Fujiwara aristocrat. Shinran went to study on Mount Hiei at the age of eight and eventually was ordained by Jien. He continued his studies on Mount Hiei for twenty years, and also visited Nara to study. But he felt increasing dissatisfaction with the path he had chosen, and when he was twenty-eight he left Mount Hiei to make a hundred-day retreat at Rokkaku-dō, in Kyoto. During this time he decided to visit Hōnen at Yoshimizu, where he became convinced that the Pure Land *nembutsu* was the practice he had been looking for and became Hōnen's disciple.

When Hōnen was exiled to Tosa in 1207, Shinran was banished to the province of Echigo (present Niigata Prefecture). During the almost five years of his exile he married the woman known as Eshinni and claimed for himself the status of "neither priest nor layman." It was then that he began to refer to himself as "foolish bald-headed Shinran." Though he was pardoned in 1211, Shinran did not return immediately to Kyoto but remained in Echigo until 1214, when he moved to Inada, in the province of Hitachi (present Ibaraki Prefecture), to propagate the *nembutsu*. He also traveled to the provinces of Shinano (present Nagano Prefecture), Shimotsuke (present Tochigi Prefecture), and Shimōsa (present Chiba Prefecture). In Inada he wrote *Kyō gyō shin shō* [Teaching, Practice, Faith, and Attainment], the summation of his thought and belief. He completed it in 1224, when he was fifty-one.

Shinran finally returned to Kyoto sometime between 1232 and 1234, though Eshinni went back to Echigo with their children. Shinran was supported in Kyoto by contributions from his disciples. It was there that the greatest tragedy of his old age occurred—the severance of relations with his son Zenran. Zenran was then in eastern Japan. Perhaps to bolster his position among the disciples, he began to claim that he and he alone had received the true teaching from Shinran and that the *nembutsu* teaching that other disciples had propagated was worthless. This of course caused an uproar among the disciples. Zenran went so far as to link himself with the authorities and persecute groups of his father's followers. Finally, in 1256, at the age of eighty-three, Shinran wrote a declaration severing all ties with Zenran. Shinran died six years later, in 1262.

While Shinran inherited the *nembutsu* teachings of Hōnen, he carried them a step further. Hōnen's teachings, based on relative dualism, advocated the rejection and transcendence of empirical reality to attain rebirth in the Pure Land. This could be achieved only by abandoning all attempts of one's own (self-power) and relying totally on Amida (other-power). Yet Hōnen also emphasized doctrines that implied effort by the believer, such as fixing one's mind on Amida and reciting the *nembutsu* in one's last moments to assure rebirth in the Pure Land. Shinran took the other-power doctrine to its logical extreme: one moment of faith, he maintained, was enough to guarantee rebirth in the Pure Land, and the true purpose of *nembutsu* recitation was not to gain rebirth there but to give thanks for salvation by Amida's power—a salvation already achieved through the fulfillment of Amida's vow. Since rebirth in the Pure Land was attained by a single moment of faith, there was no need to recite the *nembutsu* for that purpose. And since the believer was already saved, Hōnen's practice of concentrating on Amida at death was also superfluous.

Though Shinran stretched the doctrine of other-power to its limit, his was not an other-power that stood in contrast to self-power. In his doctrine of absolute other-power, the dualistic concepts of this world and the Pure Land, of ordinary people and the Buddha, were transcended. In *Kyō gyō shin shō* Shinran described the Pure Land teachings as "the perfect, complete, immediate, unobstructed, absolute, nondual teachings." He also accepted the doctrines of the identity of defilements and enlightenment, of sam-

sara and nirvana, and taught that through faith one could achieve "equality with the Buddha."

Thus with Shinran the Pure Land teachings evolved into an absolute monism that affirmed empirical reality. There are two probable reasons for this. First, as a philosophical system Hōnen's dualism compares unfavorably with the absolute monism of the Tendai doctrine of original enlightenment. Shinran, who had spent many years on Mount Hiei, obviously incorporated elements of Tendai thought into his Pure Land teachings to create an absolute monism in Pure Land terms.

The second reason has to do with the period in which Shinran was active. Hōnen taught during a time widely believed to be the period of the Decay of the Law, when rejection of this world and desire for the next were keenly felt. Shinran, however, was active in a time when people were determined to act upon the world. Yet despite Tendai philosophy's influence on Shinran, his thought remained distinct from it in at least one striking aspect: he was always deeply aware of the profound evil of the human state. His unique contribution to Buddhist thought was his discovery of the absolute, ideal realm of enlightenment within the very heart of human existence.

Dōgen (1200–1253) was born in Kyoto, the son of Inner Minister Koga Michichika. He was orphaned as a child, and it is thought that this and the complicated family relationships of the noble class into which he was born led him to enter the Buddhist Order. He received ordination on Mount Hiei at the age of thirteen but, dissatisfied with the opportunities for practice there, visited Eisai at Kennin-ji a year later. Dōgen attached himself to Myōzen, a disciple of Eisai, and in 1223 accompanied him to China. There he received the transmission of the Ts'ao-tung (Sōtō) sect of Ch'an from Chang-weng Ju-ching of Mount T'ien-t'ung, one of China's greatest Ch'an centers. He returned to Japan in 1227 and, living at Kennin-ji, wrote *Fukan zazen gi* [A Universal Recommendation of *Zazen*]. In 1231 he began writing his ninety-five-fascicle masterpiece, *Shōbōgenzō* [Treasury of the True Dharma Eye], which he did not complete until 1253, the year of his death.

Dōgen founded Kōshō-ji in Fukakusa, near Kyoto, and installed a Zen practice center in the compound. He led Zen meditation there for ten years but eventually decided to retire farther from secular entanglements and moved to Daibutsu-ji in Echizen Province (present Fukui Prefecture). Later the temple was renamed Eihei-ji, as it is known today. In 1253, gravely ill, Dōgen left the leadership of Eihei-ji to his disciple Ejō and went to Kyoto for treatment. He died there on the twenty-eighth day of the eighth month of that year.

Dōgen studied the doctrine of original enlightenment on Mount Hiei and recognized its profundity as a philosophy, but he remained dissatisfied with the actual practice of Buddhism there. The practice of seated meditation (*zazen*) became for him the essence of the way of buddhahood. He recognized the essential identity of ordinary people and the Buddha, practice and enlightenment, mind and body, and pinpointed this nondual relationship between seeming opposites as the reason that buddhahood manifests itself in human beings, that enlightenment is attained by practice, and that the mind is given concrete form in the body. With this as his philosophical base he emphasized the practice of seated meditation.

Nichiren, the last of the great Kamakura Buddhist teachers and the founder of the sect that bears his name, was born in 1222, the year after the Jōkyū Disturbance, and died in 1282, the year after the second attack by the Mongol fleet. He was born into a fishing family in the village of Kominato, on the coast of the province of Awa (present Chiba Prefecture). At the urging of his parents he entered a local Tendai temple, Kiyosumi-dera, at the age of eleven. At fifteen he was ordained by his master, Dōzembō. The next year he went to Kamakura, where he studied Pure Land and Zen teachings. After about four years he returned to Kiyosumi-dera but left almost immediately for Mount Hiei. Nichiren spent ten years on Mount Hiei in study and practice, though he made short visits to nearby Onjō-ji, Mount Kōya, and Shitennō-ji.

Nichiren was thirty-one when he arrived at some sort of religious conviction and returned once more to Kiyosumi-dera, where, on the twenty-eighth day of the fourth month of 1253, he proclaimed his newly acquired faith to an assembly. Because he strongly criticized the *nembutsu* practice, he was driven from the temple and the area by disgruntled *nembutsu* followers. He returned to Kamakura and began to spread his teachings there. When he was thirty-five, however, he confronted a serious religious question. Japan was afflicted with a series of natural and human disasters in the late 1250s, and Nichiren's question was why, since the Japanese people so fervently believed in and supported Buddhism, these evils should be visited upon them. He decided to look for an answer in the Buddhist scriptures and once again plunged into intensive study. Not only did he find the answer to his question, but also he gained new faith in the process.

That conviction was expressed in *Shugo kokka ron* [Protecting the Nation; 1259] and *Risshō ankoku ron* [Establishing the Correct Teaching and Pacifying the Nation; 1260]. In the latter he called for unifying Buddhism in Japan in accordance with the Lotus Sutra. He suggested that if all the Buddhist sects were united under a single banner, the religion would become a great force benefiting society, and he exhorted the nation's leaders to govern Japan in strict accord with a unified Buddhist ideal. Only by establishing the truth in this manner could peace be brought to the land. In this treatise Nichiren strongly criticized *nembutsu* followers in particular, whose principles and practice he regarded as antithetical to the unification of Buddhism. He presented *Risshō ankoku ron* to the government and urged its adoption. His advice was not heeded; on the contrary, he was persecuted for his criticism of the *nembutsu*. In 1261 he was exiled to the Izu Peninsula, south of Kamakura. He was released from exile in 1263, but in 1271 he was banished once again, this time to the island of Sado, in the Sea of Japan.

Nichiren was persecuted for his outspoken views throughout his life. Persecution, however, only deepened his conviction that he was a martyr for the Lotus Sutra—a bodhisattva bound to endure tribulations for the sake of the truth—and led him to emphasize more strongly than ever the bodhisattva practice of upholding the Lotus Sutra even to the point of death.

During his exile on Sado Nichiren composed his two major

works, *Kaimoku shō* [Opening the Eyes; 1272] and *Kanjin honzon shō* [The Object of Worship in Contemplation; 1273], in which he outlined the principles underlying his beliefs. He was pardoned and allowed to return to Kamakura in 1274, where he once more submitted *Risshō ankoku ron* to the government. When he saw that his advice would not be heeded, he retired to Mount Minobu, in the province of Kai (present Yamanashi Prefecture). There he composed *Senji shō* [Selecting the Time; 1275] and other works that indicated that he had decided to leave the realization of the ideal nation he envisaged to a future time.

In retirement Nichiren continued to practice the teachings of the Lotus Sutra and seems to have achieved a state of absolute freedom and transcendence that served as a comfort and a religious reward after his many years of struggle. Those years, however, and the harsh climate and spartan life of Mount Minobu, took their toll on his aging body. He set out for a hot spring in the autumn of 1282 to recuperate, but before reaching his destination he died at the home of a follower named Ikegami Munenaka, in what is now Tokyo, on the thirteenth day of the tenth month of that year.

CHAPTER NINE

Key Features of
Kamakura Buddhism

T HE NEW SECTS of Kamakura Buddhism, with the exception of those that adopted the Zen teachings introduced from China, shared certain features. Foremost was their engagement with the world. Their founders had sharply observed Japan's reality and had descended from the transcendental heights of contemplation to the empirical, relative world, where they made determined efforts to bring about the salvation of their fellow men and women.

The Kamakura Buddhist leaders sought a Buddhism suited to the capacities of their contemporaries and the time and place in which they lived. Each insisted on the importance of these considerations and used them to justify his teachings. Hōnen stated that "to practice the way of buddhahood, one must first know people's capacities well, and then the time." Shinran declared that "both priests and lay people must consider their own capacities." Nichiren proclaimed that "the Buddhist Law depends upon the time" and that "in order to study Buddhism, one must first study one's time," and urged: "With the Buddha's Eye [of Wisdom], consider the time and [people's] capacities."

All agreed that observation of people and period was crucial. What did they observe? Without exception they saw a polluted world embroiled in conflict; each of them described human capacities as deeply defiled by sin and evil. Hōnen: "The world is now in the period of the Decay of the Law, and all people are evil."

Shinran: "It is more than two thousand years since Tathagata Sha-kyamuni departed from us, and the periods of the True Law and Counterfeit Law are over. Disciples of the Tathagata left behind, lament." "As the eons decline, the bodies of sentient beings grow gradually smaller. The five pollutions and evils grow stronger, and we become like poisonous serpents or evil dragons." Dōgen: "Now is the period of the Decay of the Law, in a degenerate age. . . . In this forsaken land, during the Decay of the Law, human capacities are as different from what they were in the days of the True Law and Counterfeit Law as heaven is from earth. The rewards [of practice] are as different from those of the people in India as sand is from gold." Nichiren: "I was born more than two hundred years after we entered the period of the Decay of the Law, in a forsaken country. Further, I was of low birth, and in addition to that, poor in the practice of the Way."

The same sentiments were being expressed by representatives of the older Buddhist sects, as well. Jōkei (also known as Gedatsu Shō-nin; 1155–1213) of the Hossō school lamented: "My defilements are so profound that I am already despised in buddha-lands in the ten directions [as numerous as] the sands of the Ganges. My sins were so great that I have come to this chaotic, forsaken land, tainted with the five pollutions." The Kegon priest Kōben (also known as Myōe Shōnin; 1173–1232) wrote: "Although I am here in the human realm, it is far distant from [the time of] the Tathagata's existence in this world. Although I have encountered his teachings, I was born in a faraway, forsaken land in a degenerate age."

Neither of these priests was at all sympathetic to the new Bud-dhist movement led by Hōnen. Jōkei drafted an appeal by priests at Kōfuku-ji to have the *nembutsu* banned, which was presented to the retired emperor Gotoba in 1205. When Hōnen's *Senchaku hon-gan nembutsu shū* was made public immediately after his death in 1212, Kōben read it and in the same year composed a three-fascicle rebuttal, *Saijarin* [Breaking the Wheel of Heresy], followed the next year by another. Nevertheless, the perception of the Decay of the Law, of being an ordinary person born in a forsaken land, was common to Hōnen and his opponents. The difference was in their orientation.

The priests of the old schools looked back to the days of the True Law and to the historical Buddha, Shakyamuni, which placed them in opposition to Hōnen, who pointed to the Pure Land of Amida. Jōkei, for example, venerated relics of Shakyamuni and even chanted a "Shakyamuni *nembutsu*." He placed his hope in the appearance of Maitreya, the buddha of the future. Kōben lamented that he had not been born during the Buddha's lifetime: "There is nothing I regret more than that I was not born in the time of the Tathagata." So eager was he to encounter any trace of the Buddha that he made plans to travel to India, calculating the distance and the time it would take. (This record survives in Kōben's own hand.)

In addition to the conviction that they had been born during the period of the Decay of the Law, the leaders of the new Kamakura sects as well as many priests of the older sects and schools shared the belief that they had been born in a "forsaken" or, more literally, "peripheral" land: a land far from the scene of Shakyamuni's activities, "forsaken" by his absence, and thus one in which it was harder to achieve enlightenment.

All the Buddhist leaders of the Kamakura period showed great insight and sharp critical faculties, which they directed toward society and the human condition. On the basis of what they saw, they reinterpreted the doctrines of their religion and produced new formulations of Buddhist ideals and practice that met the needs of their age. Because each of these innovators selected and interpreted doctrines in response to the needs of the people and the time, their teachings shared the property of exclusivism. Unlike the Buddhism of earlier ages, Kamakura Buddhism did not accept all philosophies, practices, and scriptures as essentially equal. Instead, each leader selected a specific set of doctrines and practices that he regarded as the sole one appropriate to contemporary conditions.

Hōnen chose the practice of the *nembutsu*. Dōgen advocated the practice of "just sitting." While Dōgen praised the *nembutsu*, saying that "even students of Buddhism today should consider it" and remarking that one should discard miscellaneous practices and "concentrate on one practice," he was strongly critical of the *nembutsu* doctrine of rejecting this world for the Pure Land. He held that precisely because our world is one of limited empirical reality the eternal, unlimited truth is active in it, and he selected the practice of sitting in meditation as the way to practice and realize that ultimate truth. He explained practice as the manifestation of ultimate truth within empirical reality, teaching that the mind is manifest in the body and that eternal, universal truth takes form as historical reality.

In the evolution from Hōnen to Dōgen, a different attitude toward reality emerged. Whereas Hōnen sought to escape from reality and its sufferings and contradictions, Dōgen sought to engage reality. As already noted, this difference can be accounted for by the difference in the times. Dōgen was active in a period when the warrior class was forging a new social order. Of course, his age was not without signs of distress, and many of the problems of the earlier period remained unresolved. These contradictions and fluctuations required careful observation and criticism. For that reason Hōnen's rejection of empirical reality, in the form of the belief in the period of the Decay of the Law, was to be found in Dōgen's thought, too. The difference lay in their reactions more than their beliefs.

Nichiren was another Buddhist figure who, while firmly believing that the world was degenerate and human capacities feeble, located himself staunchly in the real world and endeavored to realize the ideal realm within it. Nichiren differed from Dōgen in the scope of his concern. Dōgen focused on the individual; his major concern was the subjective realization of the truth through the practice of Zen. Nichiren's vision, in contrast, was a social one. For Nichiren, realizing the ideal realm within the empirical world meant revolutionizing society by means of the True Law and creating an ideal nation—a buddha-land.

This social vision was unique to Nichiren. When he left Mount

Hiei, he still affirmed the absolute monism of the Tendai doctrine of original enlightenment; but when he saw the suffering caused by the series of disasters that occurred in the late 1250s, he began to question the state of Buddhism and the nation. Nichiren concluded that the world would not be put right until Japanese Buddhism was unified under the single truth of the Lotus Sutra and government accorded with it. *Risshō ankoku ron* was a statement of that conviction; it was this firm belief that led him repeatedly to submit the document to the shogunate.

Nichiren's warnings went unheeded, however, and he was persecuted for his views. His hut at Matsubagaya, in Kamakura, was burned; he was exiled to Izu; on his return home he was set upon by an armed band at a place called Komatsubara; and finally he was exiled to the island of Sado. These persecutions, however, only strengthened his resolve, turning him into a religious militant who battled secular authority. He also became a prophet who delivered repeated warnings about the future awaiting a nation and people that ignored his reproaches. Events conspired to encourage Nichiren's inclination to prophecy. His predictions of calamity seemed to come true as the Hōjō regency continued to be afflicted with power struggles and revolts; and a national crisis approached with the arrival of Mongol envoys in 1268 and 1269 demanding Japan's submission, followed by attempted invasions by Mongol fleets in 1274 and 1281.

Nichiren came to see himself as a martyr to the truth and began to emphasize the bodhisattva practice taught in the Lotus Sutra, which encourages total devotion to the sutra, even to the point of giving one's life for it. This message appears most clearly in the section of the sutra from chapter 10, "A Teacher of the Law," to chapter 22, "The Final Commission." Those who strive to uphold the truth and realize the ideal world of the Lotus Sutra, enduring all sufferings and difficulties (represented by the bodhisattvas springing up out of the earth), are identified as messengers of the Buddha. They are encouraged to continue with their bodhisattva practice without fearing the reprisals that are sure to come. Nichiren began to focus on this portion of the Lotus Sutra during his exile on Sado and to refer to himself as "a practitioner of the Lotus Sutra," meaning one committed to the bodhisattva practice, fearlessly battling the evil in the world while struggling to realize the ideal realm.

The Lotus Sutra has three main themes, treated in three different parts of the scripture. The first part teaches that the universe is unified in the wonderful Law of the One Vehicle (the teaching of the Lotus Sutra). The second part proclaims that the Buddha—the principle of enlightenment—is eternal. The third part states that bodhisattvas, whose practice is to endure hardships and to give their lives for the sutra, are messengers of the Eternal Buddha. This part emphasizes the activity of human beings in the empirical world (bodhisattva practice), and teaches that when the universal truth of the Lotus Sutra takes that form it becomes an exclusive practice with tremendous power to change the world. The ultimate intent of the Lotus Sutra can be read in its emphasis on bodhisattva practice. Nichiren's hardships led him to discover this theme, which was so important to him that he called his teaching "the third teaching," alluding to the sutra's third great theme.

Shinran, too, actively engaged the world of empirical reality. Inheriting Hōnen's otherworldly *nembutsu*, he made it a thing of this world. While lamenting the profound evil of the human condition, he taught the attainment of an absolute realm in the midst of empirical reality through the *nembutsu*. For him the *nembutsu* existed within the human realm, yet at the same time was the expression of the joy and love that resulted from being enveloped in the absolute love of Amida. The more constricted our reality, the greater our chance of attaining the absolute state of oneness with Amida and the joy bound to well up within us when we achieve it.

In his *Jōdo wasan* [Pure Land Hymns] Shinran wrote: "'The person who rejoices in faith / Is equal to the Tathagata,' says [the Buddha]. / Great faith is the buddha-nature / And the buddha-nature is the Tathagata." The dichotomies of this world and the next, of the Saha-world and the Pure Land, of ordinary people and the Buddha, were not problems for Shinran because he believed that those with true faith were already in the Pure Land and one with the Buddha. The Buddha abode was not in some far-away Pure Land of enlightenment or future world but could be found throughout the universe: "The Tathagata is everywhere in the infinite worlds. In other words, he is in the minds of the sea of living beings, and in all plants and the material world as well: all will attain buddhahood."

The rejection of empirical reality, the critical approach and active engagement evidenced by the leaders of Kamakura Buddhism, led to resistance to established political authority, and they found themselves on the side of the people in opposition to the establishment. For this reason Kamakura Buddhism is often described as a Buddhism of the people.

Hōnen strongly emphasized the needs of the common people as one of his reasons for singling out recitation of the *nembutsu* as the sole "easy practice" and advocating the abandonment of all other practices. In his *Senchaku hongan nembutsu shū* he declared: "All sentient beings are equally born in the Pure Land." He paid special attention to the lower classes and recognized that for them such "good works" as commissioning the construction of Buddhist images and pagodas were impossible; for them he preached the "easy practice" of the *nembutsu:* "Long ago, when Amida Tathagata was the *bhikshu* [male member of the Order] Dharmakara, he was possessed by equal compassion for all beings, and to embrace all of them he made his Original Vow, by which we are reborn in the Pure Land, not because we build Buddhist images or temples but only because we engage in the sole practice of reciting the *nembutsu.*"

When Hōnen was exiled to Tosa Province at the age of seventy-four, his disciples were worried about his health and urged him to compromise with the authorities, but he declared that his exile was all that he could wish for, since it provided him with an ideal chance to preach the *nembutsu* to peasants. Hōnen's special attention to the oppressed and despised classes, and to women in particular, is recorded with great frequency in biographies of him. He insisted that there were no restrictions on the Buddha's compassion and that noble and lowly alike were ordinary human beings. His belief in the equality of all people and his special concern with extending the Buddha's salvation to the lowest classes exemplified a Buddhism of the people, even if it stopped short of a plan for revolution and political freedom.

Shinran inherited Hōnen's belief in equality and taught that the Buddha's salvation was available to both the virtuous and the wicked, the high and the low. Shinran, too, paid special heed to those who were scorned as having as little value as "stones, clay tiles, pebbles." His exile to Echigo Province brought the poor country people of the outlying regions to his attention and drew him even closer to the common people.

Though both Hōnen and Shinran were of distinguished birth, neither was the least condescending to his fellows. They placed themselves on the same level, always including themselves in their descriptions of those of low estate: "ordinary, ignorant beings like us" (Hōnen); "we, like stones, clay tiles, pebbles" (Shinran). Hōnen called himself "Hōnembō of the ten evils, ignorant Hōnembō," and Shinran is well known for describing himself as "neither priest nor layman" and as "foolish bald-headed Shinran." In Shinran's self-descriptions, in particular, can be detected a tone of resistance to the priests and political authorities, who so prided themselves on their temporal power. Shinran himself stated that his chosen cognomens were intended to express his anger and to protest the abuse of power that had sent Hōnen and him into exile.

Because Dōgen emphasized the merits of the Buddhist Order, he is often thought of as upholding the superiority of the clergy to the laity. But in fact his emphasis on the Order was a form of protest against its corruption. Since the clergy had become so closely linked to authority, Dōgen's call for reform was also a protest against secular power. He revived the old debate, which had originated in China, over whether the clergy was above secular authority. He subscribed to the doctrine that priests need not bow before rulers, "because the virtues of members of the Buddhist Order are superior." The reason he retired to the mountains of Echizen Province was to remove himself from the arena of power.

Dōgen's critical attitude toward authority aligned him with the common people. He asserted that the Order included all believers, without distinction between clergy and laity. He sharply criticized clericalism and those who took false pride in, for example, remaining celibate. Dōgen took a clear stand on discrimination against women, as well, and strongly condemned the practice of prohibiting women from entering certain temple compounds (such as those on Mount Kōya), for he believed that all people of both sexes are equal: "The buddhas and the patriarchs were all originally ordinary people. . . . There is no reason to look down on yourself as being foolish and dull."

The strongest opposition to secular power was shown by Nichiren. He held high the standard of the sacred authority of the Buddhist Law and confronted secular authority from that standpoint. Nichiren is often referred to as a nationalist, but there can be no greater error. He wrote so frequently of the Japanese nation because he wished to destroy secular authority and revolutionize Japan to accord with the Buddhist Law: "Nothing surpasses the Law of the Buddha for understanding the rise and fall of the nation." "The Buddha is the great ruler, the *kami* his ministers." "The Law of the Buddha is the body, this world its mere shadow. When the body bends, the shadow falls over."

Though the *honji suijaku* theory does appear in Nichiren's writings, he used it to support the authority of the Buddha as the origin of Japan's *kami*—that is, to deny the authority of the Shintō deities. Nichiren taught that one who trusts in the Buddha transcends the authority of the *kami* and the ruler, and he strongly warned his followers against affiliating themselves with secular power. He made the same claim for himself: "Since I am the messenger of the lord of the teaching, Shakyamuni, Amaterasu Ōmikami and Hachiman should bow to me, place their hands together, and bend to the ground." "Nichiren is the father and mother of today's rulers." When he retired to Mount Minobu, however, he left the establishment of the ideal society he envisioned to a future time, reposing in a realm that transcended the petty quarrels of the world. As he wrote in *Senji shō:* "Though, born in the ruler's realm, I must follow his dictates in my actions, I do not have to follow them in my belief."

Nichiren's refusal to recognize the legitimacy of any secular power, and his insistence that those who have faith in the Lotus Sutra, however lowly their social status, transcend the authority of the state and the indigenous *kami*, allied him strongly with the common people, as seen in his referring to himself as "a child of the common people."

Much more could be written about Buddhist activities during the Kamakura period. There were, for example, several priests of the Nara schools, besides those already mentioned, who should be noted—in particular Eizon (also known as Shien Shōnin and Kō-shō Bosatsu; 1201–90) and his disciple Ninshō (also known as Ryōkambō; 1217–1303), who performed good works and endeavored to revive the fortunes of the Ritsu school. Numerous priests lamented the collapse of morals among both the clergy and the general populace and attempted to reinstate the Buddhist precepts. But Eizon and Ninshō combined insistence on the formal rules of discipline and morality with true self-discipline, stressing the control of one's own desires. This they demonstrated in the practice of good works for the benefit of society, such as aid to the poor, care for lepers, and prohibitions against the taking of life. Ninshō applied himself so enthusiastically to these tasks that he was known as a "living buddha."

Whether they belonged to the old schools or the new sects, the Kamakura Buddhist reformers sought the ultimate truth and, though their methods differed, gave it form in their teachings and practice.

CHAPTER TEN

The Triumph of the Secular

B EFORE REVIEWING the development of Buddhism in medieval
Japan—the late Kamakura period, the brief Northern and
Southern Courts period (1336–92), the Muromachi period (1392–
1568), and the Momoyama period (1568–1603)—let us examine
the changes that were taking place in Japanese political, cultural,
and intellectual life. One important development was a gradual
change in the power structure that governed Japan. Central authority began to weaken as powerful regional lords grew more and
more independent and built up their own military forces. These
lords devoted their energies to consolidating, ruling, and augment-
ing their holdings. At the same time, agricultural technology made
significant progress, resulting in improved production and a higher
standard of living for the peasantry. Surplus agricultural products
could be taken to market and sold, and a class of merchants arose
to oversee this commerce. With the growth of trade, roads and
towns developed. But more important, for the first time the common people gained a position of some respect as the importance
of production and distribution was recognized. This development
led to the rise of a popular, life-affirming culture with humanistic
values.

Popular performing arts exemplified the new cultural mood. One
such art was Sarugaku. Eventually refined into the elegant dance-
drama of Noh by Kan'ami (1333–84) and his son Zeami (1363–

1443), Sarugaku had been imported from T'ang China, where it was known as a "miscellaneous entertainment," in contrast to "formal entertainment." In other words, it was a popular or vulgar genre. In Japan, Sarugaku was performed at shrine and temple festivals as a humorous entertainment that included acrobatic stunts and comic mimicry of animals and people. It was an entertainment of the common people, initially scorned by the nobility as "beggars' play." But it grew in popularity, and Kan'ami and Zeami, Sarugaku actors of low birth, enjoyed the patronage of the shogunate.

Zeami wrote a famous treatise on the aesthetics of Noh, *Fūshi kaden,* and introduced elements from Japan's classical literature into the genre, but its humble origins remain clear. Noh depicts the feelings of ordinary human beings as they fluctuate between joy and sorrow. The presence of vengeful spirits in Noh is another sign of its popular origins. Buddhist sentiments of transience are also frequently expressed in Noh plays, but always in the context of the situations of the characters depicted.

The *nembutsu odori* (*nembutsu* dance) was another popular entertainment. It evolved from dancing while chanting or singing the *nembutsu,* a method of worship taught by Ippen (1239–89), the founder of the Ji sect of Pure Land Buddhism, as a means of propagating the *nembutsu* and Pure Land teachings among the people. As it spread, this form of dancing became a secular entertainment. (The dances that are still performed in Japan at the time of the Bon festival in midsummer are believed to derive from *nembutsu odori*.) In the Muromachi period the upper classes enthusiastically took it up, and high and low alike donned extravagant costumes to perform *nembutsu odori*. Most of those professionally involved in Sarugaku and *nembutsu odori* were followers of the Ji sect. This is apparent in such names as Kan'ami and Zeami, which incorporate part of the name Amida.

In the Muromachi period many activities were cultivated and developed beyond their original functions into arts: the tea ceremony (*sadō* or *chadō*), flower arrangement (*ikebana*), and incense appreciation (*kōdō*) are prime examples. As Eisai's famous work *Kissa yōjō ki* [Tea Drinking for the Cultivation of Life; 1211] attests, tea was first appreciated for its medicinal properties. Only later was it drunk for its taste, and finally its preparation was developed into a ceremonial social function. Flower arrangement had its origins in the decoration of Buddhist altars. Gradually its religious import lessened and it was practiced to beautify daily life and, eventually, as an aesthetic pursuit in its own right.

The same tendency toward aestheticization was seen in medieval painting and architecture. Ink paintings, for example, were originally the work of Zen priests, and Zen personages or anecdotes were frequently their subjects, making them, in a sense, religious paintings. But in the Muromachi period landscapes and other secular subjects were increasingly depicted, even by Zen priests. The works of Sesshū (1420–1506), a Zen priest who traveled to China to study ink painting, and Sesson (ca. 1504–ca. 1589) exemplify this trend.

The *shoin* style of architecture, which included such distinctive features as the decorative alcove (*tokonoma*), staggered shelves (*chigaidana*), and the built-in desk called a *shoin,* for which the style was named, derived from religious structures—in particular, priests' quarters. In the Muromachi period this style was adapted to secular architecture. The *tokonoma* is especially representative of the aestheticism of the Muromachi period, for it was in this alcove that paintings, flowers, and tea utensils were displayed.

If the arts of Muromachi derived from Buddhism, their influence was also returned to its source. The famous rock-and-sand gardens of the Zen temples Ryōan-ji and the Daitoku-ji subtemple Daisen-in, in Kyoto, are fine examples. While these gardens are meant to symbolize the most profound insights of Zen, they are also aesthetic achievements to be appreciated for the great artistic skill that is evident in the way they are able to suggest the huge expanse of nature in a modest space. Ink paintings depicting vast and varied landscapes in black and white and the tiny two- or three-mat confines of the tea room, meanwhile, suggest the underlying principle of Zen, which is to cast off the confines of this world and enter directly and immediately into the truth. They exhibit a transcendental mood and keen spirituality.

Yet for all their religious suggestiveness, the guiding concepts of the arts of medieval Japan—the spirit of quiet simplicity (*wabi*) cultivated in the tea ceremony, the *sukiya*-style architecture (a variant of the *shoin* style) of the tea room, the "mystery" (*yūgen*) and aesthetic melancholy (*sabi*) of poetry—were primarily aesthetic principles, though they might achieve their goal by an apparent denial of beauty and elegance. The *sukiya*-style architecture of the tea room, for example, seems at first glance to be simple and natural, but in fact its materials have been cleverly chosen and manipulated to produce an extremely sophisticated effect.

The arts of medieval Japan developed and spread in the context of the daily life of the people, and as these arts were refined, their enjoyment and appreciation became a pastime of the Japanese in general. The arts of the medieval period—Japan's Renaissance, in some ways—affirmed life, sang the praises of the world, and aimed to bring pleasure; and Japanese Buddhism evolved in response to this spirit.

It is widely held that the foundation of Japanese culture and art as we know them today was laid in the Muromachi period. In that regard we must note that this period was also a time of systematization in Japanese intellectual life, and that this systematization contributed to the development of culture and art. It was Buddhist practice that supplied the apparatus for the systematization of both thought and art. One striking example is the oral transmission (*kuden*) of the secrets of an art. Oral transmission was originally the means by which the Tendai doctrine of original enlightenment was passed from master to disciple, and the tradition of the oral transmission of essential teachings soon spread to other sects of Buddhism and to Shintō. In imitation of this practice, secret oral transmission from master to disciple evolved in many of the arts, as well.

Though Buddhism was instrumental in the process of systematization, it had to be assimilated and adapted before it could be applied in other fields. At times, all Buddhist coloring was discarded. One example is the Unique Shintō (Yuiitsu Shintō) of Yoshida Kanetomo (1435–1511). This form of Shintō, developed by Ryō-hen (1196–1252), Jihen (fl. 1333–40), and the courtier and scholar Kitabatake Chikafusa (1293–1354), was given its definitive formulation by Kanetomo. Ryōhen was a priest on Mount Hiei who later turned to Shintō. Jihen, also a Mount Hiei priest who converted to Shintō, belonged to the same family as Yoshida Kanetomo (Jihen is said to have been the brother of Yoshida Kenkō, the author of *Tsurezuregusa*). As a result, their writings on Shintō subjects were strongly influenced by the Tendai doctrine of original enlightenment.

The mature doctrine of Unique Shintō propounded by Kanetomo rejected the preeminence of Buddhism and claimed that the Shintō deities were primary—the essence—and the Buddhist deities only their manifestations. Kanetomo also reversed the traditional view of the superiority of India and China to Japan and established the hallowed Shintō virtues of sincerity (*shōjiki*) and purity as primary, making the Buddhist virtue of compassion secondary.

In *Kyūji honki gengi* [The Profound Meaning of the Imperial History of Ancient Events] Jihen wrote: "Japan is the root of the three realms, and in other countries you will find only Japan's traces. Japan is the sprout from the seed. . . . The essence is in our divine land. T'ang [China] has grasped the branches and leaves and India has obtained the fruit. But when the flower falls, it returns to the roots." This was later known as the doctrine of roots, foliage, flowers, and fruit. A work by Kanetomo, though attributed by him to his ancestor Kanenobu, *Yuiitsu Shintō myōbō yōshū* [An Anthology of the Doctrines of Unique Shintō], expresses the same idea: "Japan produces the root. The foliage comes forth in China, and the flowers and fruit in India. Thus Buddhism is the flower and fruit of all teachings, Confucianism the branches and leaves, and Shintō the root. The two teachings [Buddhism and Confucianism] are merely emanations of Shintō."

Jihen, in *Toyoashihara jimpū waki* [Harmonious Record of the Ways of the *Kami* of Japan; 1340], identified the Shintō virtues of

sincerity and purity as primary and the Buddhist virtue of compassion as their manifestation. He explained that Shintō teachings
were no longer properly understood and that therefore in this "latter age" the Shintō truth was taught in the provisional form of the
Buddha's compassion. Shintō virtues are also set above Buddhist
compassion in Kitabatake Chikafusa's *Jinnō shōtō ki* [The True
Lineage of the Divine Sovereigns]. Chikafusa attributed certain
virtues to the three sacred objects of Shintō: the mirror is the original source of sincerity, the jewel the source of compassion, and
the sword the source of wisdom. The mirror being the primary sacred object, Chikafusa clearly established sincerity as the primary
virtue.

As we have seen, the Muromachi period was a time of systematization in the arts, as well. *Fūshi kaden,* Zeami's treatise on Noh
aesthetics, is a prime example of this trend. Though his subject
was Noh, Zeami had much to say about aesthetics and the philosophy of art in general. In this work he outlined a scheme of artistic
development consisting of three stages: *jo* (introduction), *ha* (breaking), and *kyū* (rushing). Zeami's scheme was adopted in the art of
flower arrangement, as well. One of the first written records of
ikebana teachings, the late-fifteenth-century *Sendenshō* [The Transmission of the Sages], articulated the principles of *shin* (formal
style), *gyō* (semiformal style), and *sō* (informal style) in terms of
Zeami's *jo, ha,* and *kyū.* In the art of the tea ceremony, these principles were expressed as *shu* (preserving), *ha* (breaking), and *ri* (transcending).

Jo (or *shu*) means to begin by establishing the form of the work.
Ha means to break that form. The last element, *kyū,* means to pursue the "breaking" to its natural end, or to "rush" the *ha* to its culmination. *Ri,* or transcending, suggests leaving behind the broken
form and entering a new realm. A famous anecdote about the
great tea master Sen no Rikyū (1522–91) illustrates the development of the scheme of *shu, ha,* and *ri.* Rikyū's master ordered him
to sweep the garden of a teahouse. When Rikyū went into the garden, he found it immaculate. He immediately realized his master's

intent and reached up to shake a tree branch, scattering several leaves along the garden path.

The Japanese perceived movement and beauty in the natural process of the blossoming of flowers, their withering, and the falling of leaves in autumn, a theme we have already explored in chapter 4. Zeami stated that "it is the withering of the flower that is especially attractive"; and Yoshida Kenkō, in *Tsurezuregusa*, remarked: "The most precious thing in life is its uncertainty." He also wrote: "Are we to look at cherry blossoms only in full bloom, the moon only when it is cloudless?"[1] This current of Japanese thought is found in the earliest literary sources, but in the Muromachi period it was articulated in a systematic fashion for the first time, becoming the basis for the development of many different arts. The famous words of the twelfth-generation master of the Ikenobō school of flower arrangement, Senkei, express that sentiment: "Arrange together flowers from past and present, far and near." "Past and present" refers to flowers of differing seasons; "far and near" means arranging the flowers three-dimensionally. Senkei's words thus identified the ultimate goal of the art of *ikebana* as the expression of change in both time and space. This formulation of the art of *ikebana* encapsulates one of the ideals of Japanese thought.

Systematization also fostered the salient characteristics of Muromachi culture, affirmation of life and praise of this world. While Yoshida Kenkō wrote of the mingled pathos (*mono no aware*) and fascination inherent in the pageant of change in both the natural world and human life, he also remarked: "People who hate death should love life. How is it possible for men not to rejoice each day over the pleasure of being alive?"[2] And quoting a wealthy man as saying, "It isn't worth living if you are poor. Only the rich man merits the name of 'man,'"[3] he acknowledged the worth of that pursuit. (This passage was frequently cited in collections of max-

1. Keene, *Essays in Idleness*, p. 115.
2. Ibid., p. 79.
3. Ibid., p. 178.

ims for merchants of the Edo period [1603–1868].) In short, two prevailing trends of thought were systematized and articulated in the Muromachi period: belief in harmony with nature and affirmation of humanity and this world.

Affirmation of humanity led to the seemingly contradictory phenomenon called in Japanese *gekokujō*, or revolt from below. Such revolts occurred with increasing frequency in medieval Japan as regional landowners asserted rule over their territories and called themselves daimyō—literally, "great name." At the same time, wealthy peasants and merchants emerged. The age was one of rivalry for power. Culture was created by the powerful and the successful, and thought was distinguished by a practical, secular bent.

Massive castles were built as a proud declaration of the power and authority of the daimyō. The great castles of the sixteenth-century warlords Oda Nobunaga (1534–82) at Azuchi and Toyotomi Hideyoshi (1537–98) at Osaka and at Fushimi, in Kyoto, no longer exist in their original form, but extant Himeji Castle, in what is now Hyōgo Prefecture, provides a hint of their splendor. The castle rooms were adorned with paintings of giant trees, gorgeous flowers and other plants, and fierce birds and beasts. Confucianism provided the ideological theme for the keep. In Azuchi Castle, for example, paintings of Confucian kings and sages dominated the seventh, and highest, level of the keep, while paintings of Shakyamuni at the time of his enlightenment and of his ten great disciples were relegated to the sixth level. Two painters of the Kanō school, Eitoku (1543–90) and Sanraku (1559–1635), were the main artists responsible. As their extant works show, their paintings, in gold leaf and rich colors, were full of vigor.

Nobunaga and Hideyoshi, each of whom in turn made himself the de facto ruler of Japan, felt no awe of the *kami* and buddhas and even sought to elevate themselves to an equal plane. According to the writings of the Jesuit Luis Frois (1532–97), who lived in Japan from 1563 until his death, Nobunaga publicly proclaimed himself a living deity and ruler of the world, while the Jesuit Jean Crasset, in his 1689 history of Christianity in Japan, noted that

Hideyoshi wished to be deified after his death and to be worshiped as the great champion of Japan.

In that age of struggle, when warriors often risked death, constant awareness of and preparation for death were necessary. The great warlords, who witnessed the rise and fall of their friends and foes and sudden reversals of power, felt keenly the impermanence of human life and achievement. Nobunaga is said to have recited frequently the poem "A human life lasts fifty years. / Compared with the heavens / It is like a dream. / Once born, / Is there anyone who shall not die?" He was also fond of the verse "Death is certain. / What should the grass by the roadside do? / Leave behind the tale of that certainty." Hideyoshi's deathbed poem reflects similar sentiments: "My existence: / It settled like dew / And now like dew evaporates. / All is nothing more / Than the dream of a dream." But though Nobunaga and Hideyoshi expressed and no doubt felt these sentiments, they did not direct their gaze to some far-off eternal world that held the secret of human life. Instead, they accepted the inevitability of death and lived life to the full. From a Buddhist point of view, this may have been the height of arrogance and folly, but at that time it was a common attitude.

Buddhism responded to the changing currents of thought in medieval Japan by adapting its teachings to come to terms with the rise in the general standard of living and people's vigorous pursuit of worldly benefits. Part of the Buddhist response was the increasing importance placed on magical practices of esoteric Buddhism, worship of folk deities, and prayers for practical benefits and worldly success. In the Tendai sect, for example, the doctrine of original enlightenment was now interpreted as a total affirmation of human life just as it is. All daily activities were regarded as Buddhist practice, the laity came to be regarded as superior to the clergy, and the Shintō deities were identified as the divine essence, the buddhas and bodhisattvas their manifestations.

In both the Tendai and Shingon sects, secret practices developed that included sexual intercourse as a way to attain enlightement. In Tendai this practice, known as "taking refuge in the secret teachings" (*genshi kimyō dan*), was transmitted in the Ekōbō branch in particular; in Shingon, the Tachikawa school taught that man and woman, yang and yin, could be likened to the two great Shingon mandalas (the Diamond Realm and Womb Realm mandalas), and that their union would lead to enlightenment in this life. Secret Tendai and Shingon rituals also found their way into the Jōdo and Jōdo Shin sects.

The adoption of secular morality in the Jōdo Shin sect is already evident in the writings of Kakunyo (1270–1351), the third-generation chief abbot of the sect's head temple, Hongan-ji, in Kyoto. In his *Kaijashō* [Reforming Heresy], he identified the five major Buddhist precepts (not to kill, steal, indulge in sexual misconduct, lie, or drink intoxicants) with the secular virtues of benevolence, righteousness, courtesy, wisdom, and faith and enjoined believers to cultivate the latter.

In the Nichiren sect (also known as the Hokke, or Lotus, sect for the primacy given to the Lotus Sutra) the influence of the Tendai doctrine of original enlightenment grew greatly after Nichiren's death, leading to a strong emphasis on the essential identity of defilements and enlightenment. The active engagement with empirical reality that Nichiren had taught became simple affirmation of the world, and prayers for practical benefits and the fulfillment of worldly desires began to appear in the sect's practices, as did the worship of folk deities, such as Kishimojin, the thirty guardian deities, and Daikoku.

During the lifetime of the Sōtō priest Keizan Jōkin (1268–1325), esoteric Buddhist and secular influences grew in that sect, as well. In *Keizan shingi* [The Pure Regulations of Keizan], the regular recitation of prayers to prevent disaster and induce good fortune is included in the Sōtō calendar of religious observances. Deities of India and China are invoked, together with Japan's indigenous deities, and divination and other folk practices are included in the regulations. *Denkō roku* [The Transmission of the Light], a collection of Keizan's discourses, emphasizes loyalty to the nation's ruler, filial piety, and respect for secular morality.

Around the same time, the Rinzai priest Kokan Shiren (1278–

1346) wrote *Genkō shakusho* [Genkō-era History of Buddhism], the first comprehensive history of Japanese Buddhism, wherein he criticized Myōhen (1141–1224), a priest who had retired to Mount Kōya and had become known as "the Holy Man of Mount Kōya." Kokan attacked Myōhen for escapism and for lack of filial piety. The Rinzai sect, incidentally, enjoyed the patronage of the shogunate and greatly augmented its power. In the Muromachi period the sect grew wealthy from land and trade revenues (it largely controlled the China trade) and even ventured into the moneylending business. With the increased wealth of the temples, the priests' standard of living improved and they could concentrate on religious practice free from mundane worries. Such was their leisure that they were able to produce the literature known as *gozan bungaku,* or "writings from the five mountains," a reference to the five major Rinzai Zen temples of Kyoto and the five of Kamakura.

All these developments indicate the secularization of Buddhism. From a religious standpoint, it may have been a regrettable development. The very trends that the leaders of Kamakura Buddhism had warned against and had criticized so strongly had triumphed. But however secularized the Buddhists became, some at least preserved a final bastion from which they would not retreat. Kakunyo's son Zonkaku (1290–1373) wrote in *Shoshin honkai shū* [The True Wishes of the *Kami*]: "Japan, as the nation of the *kami,* still enjoys the full effect of the *kami*'s magical powers." But he did not abandon the position that the Buddhist deities were primary and the indigenous *kami* secondary. Zonkaku also preached against the worship of folk *kami.* He allowed the worship of the great clan deities, who were regarded as having contributed to the building of the nation and who had been identified as bodhisattvas or as manifestations of buddhas. These were "good" deities, who safeguarded the Buddhist teachings and rejoiced at devotees of the *nembutsu,* so their worship was permissible, but Zonkaku asserted that it was unnecessary to worship at Shintō shrines. He also defended the superiority of Buddhist compassion to Shintō virtues: "The *kami* will not accept those with erroneous views even if their bodies are purified. But the *kami* will protect even those who are impure if they show compassion."

Yet the majority of Buddhists walked the secular road. Though they may deserve criticism for this, their efforts to respond to the energy and activity of the populace must not be overlooked. Two excellent examples of the bond between religion and the common people are found in the Jōdo Shin sect, which spread in peasant communities and became involved in peasant uprisings, and the Nichiren sect, which made many converts among urban merchants and played an important part in their struggle for autonomy.

The *shōen*, or manor, system of absentee land management and taxation that had prevailed in the Heian period began to decline in the late Kamakura period. As it weakened, local landowners grasped power in some areas, while in others peasants formed self-governing communities. Occasionally, when their communities were threatened, peasants took up weapons in their own defense. The Jōdo Shin sect took hold in many of these communities, partly because the sect's teachings were propagated not from above by a clerical elite but by lay believers—an organizational structure that resembled that of the self-governing peasant communities and thus contributed to the sect's success in penetrating them.

To the eighth-generation chief abbot of Hongan-ji, Rennyo (1415–99), belongs much of the credit for the success of this expansion. Rennyo began his efforts to spread the faith in the northwestern part of Honshū upon his arrival in Yoshizaki, in the province of Echizen, in 1471, acquiring many followers in that region. Yoshizaki became a center of *nembutsu* practice, attracting believers not only from the surrounding area but also from farther afield. At one time a small city of *nembutsu* followers grew up. It was easy for this concentration of like-minded individuals to make use of their religious organization for political purposes, and some groups of *nembutsu* followers—peasants in particular, who were especially hard pressed by the feudal authorities—rose in revolts known as *ikkō ikki*, or single-minded uprisings, because of the participants' single-minded faith in Amida. *Ikkō ikki* occurred around Japan, the largest being one in the province of Kaga (present

Ishikawa Prefecture) in 1488. The lord of Kaga, Togashi Masachika, was forced to commit suicide, and Jōdo Shin followers ruled the region for nearly a century.

Of course this resistance to established authority called down the wrath of both the Buddhist establishment on Mount Hiei and the ruling warrior class. Hongan-ji was attacked and burned by warrior-priests from Mount Hiei, but Rennyo rebuilt the temple in Yamashina, west of Kyoto, and in his writings continued to instruct his followers in the proper form of the faith and the rules they should obey.

Actually, the doctrines of the Jōdo Shin sect had no direct bearing on the peasant uprisings, though an indirect effect can be detected. That was believers' conviction that they were assured of rebirth in the Pure Land, a conviction that enabled them to take up arms with no fear of death. Another contributing factor was the egalitarian nature of their faith and its organization, which helped meld believers into communities willing to defy the authorities.

The Nichiren sect drew its believers not from the peasants but from prosperous city merchants and artisans, known collectively as *machishū*. Nichiren Buddhism was especially widespread among the *machishū* of Kyoto; at one time almost the entire *machishū* population belonged to the sect. Nichizō (1269–1342), a second-generation disciple of Nichiren, began to spread his master's teachings in Kyoto in the spring of 1294, quickly winning the patronage of the *machishū*. The merchants of the Sanjō, Shijō, and Shichijō districts, the weavers, and the parishioners of the Gion and Inari shrines all became Nichiren followers.

Just as peasants formed self-governing communities, so the *machishū* formed militias to protect their communities. The priests of Mount Hiei were jealous of the success of the Nichiren sect among the Kyoto townspeople, and on more than one occasion they attacked and burned Nichiren temples in the capital. The armed uprisings in defense of Nichiren temples in Kyoto were called *hokke ikki*, or lotus uprisings. When Jōdo Shin communities spread to the capital region, there were also occasional clashes between Jōdo Shin and Nichiren followers.

Since the Rinzai Zen sect had the support of the shogunate, at first it enjoyed the greatest power and authority in Kyoto, but by about 1400 it was followed closely by the Nichiren sect, and by about 1460 Nichiren followers dominated the capital. In 1440 there were already sixty Nichiren temples in Kyoto, twenty-one of which ranked as "main temples," with branch temples under their jurisdiction. The Nichiren followers who accompanied the warrior Hosokawa Harumoto to burn Hongan-ji in 1532 numbered ten thousand on foot and more than four hundred on horseback. The procession filled the streets of Kyoto. Until the Nichiren sect was dealt a fatal blow in an attack by Mount Hiei forces in 1536, it was the de facto ruler of the capital.

The Kyoto *machishū* were attracted to the Nichiren sect because the active attitude of Nichiren and his disciples toward the world had much in common with the entrepreneurial spirit. The spread of Nichiren Buddhism in the capital is an outstanding example of the combination of practical and spiritual benefits that character-ized Buddhism in medieval Japan.

CHAPTER ELEVEN

The Subjugation of Buddhism

BUDDHISM EXPANDED its role in medieval Japan by making a place for itself in the life of the common people, and the Buddhist sects founded in the Kamakura period developed into large institutions. There was a danger, though, in the intimate relationship between Buddhism and everyday life, for the religion was easily tainted by the vaulting ambitions that characterized the age. Kamakura Buddhism had been characterized by rejection of secular authority in favor of the higher claims of the religious spirit, an attitude that entailed not only a critique of material desires and the lust for power but also an egalitarianism that sometimes led to a revolutionary drive to overturn the society of discrimination between rich and poor, aristocrat and commoner. The Buddhism of the Muromachi period, however, achieved the opposite result: in its attempt to keep pace with popular mores, it was lured into the whirlpool of secular desires and ambitions and in the end was engulfed by them.

The original intent of the peasant and merchant uprisings described in the previous chapter was to preserve the community's way of life and defend its right to self-government. Gradually, however, religious groups were caught up in the turbulent struggle for control of the provinces, and their little communities became fodder for the powerful daimyō as they expanded their territories and established domains over which they exercised absolute rule. During the part of the Muromachi period known as the Age of the Warring Provinces (1467–1568) the daimyō battled incessantly among themselves. The winners of the contest—Oda Nobunaga, Toyotomi Hideyoshi, and Tokugawa Ieyasu (1542–1616)—successively claimed the status of national ruler. Tokugawa forces decisively defeated Toyotomi forces in the battle of Sekigahara in 1600, and in 1603 Ieyasu established the Tokugawa shogunate, which was to rule Japan for the 265 years of the Edo period (so called because the shogunal government was located in Edo, present Tokyo)—a prodigious length of time for any regime.

Buddhism, whether of the older schools and sects or of the sects founded in the Kamakura period, fell victim to the ambition of the feudal lords, was used by them, was attacked by them, was defeated and regulated by them, and finally was domesticated by them. Though the Edo period offered much of value in cultural and intellectual achievement, from a religious standpoint it was an age of decline. Buddhism became increasingly secularized and, despite occasional bursts of vigor, lost its vitality and settled quietly into the grave it had dug for itself.

The first step in the secular authorities' domination of Buddhism was taken by Nobunaga when he defeated the warrior-priests of Enryaku-ji in battle on Mount Hiei. In the ninth month of 1571 his forces burned most of Enryaku-ji to the ground, destroying a great many treasures. Several thousand men and women are said to have died in the assault. Next he attacked Mount Kōya and the Nara temple of Kōfuku-ji. All temples that would not pledge allegiance to him were burned. He also launched an attack on Hongan-ji, which was now in Ishiyama (present Osaka), but the eleventh-generation chief abbot, Kennyo (1543–92), allied himself with anti-Nobunaga daimyō and withstood Nobunaga's assaults for eleven years. In the third month of 1580 a peace pact was concluded, but when Kennyo left Hongan-ji, Nobunaga's forces burned it.

Nobunaga, concerned over the Nichiren sect's intransigence, combative propagation methods, and growing popularity in his castle town of Azuchi, ordered a debate between representatives of the Nichiren and Jōdo sects in 1579. This event, which took place

at Azuchi Castle, was part of Nobunaga's plan to destroy the
Nichiren sect. The Nichiren priests were declared the losers and
either imprisoned or executed, and the sect was made to pay
Nobunaga a heavy fine.

Hideyoshi, who succeeded Nobunaga as the de facto ruler of
Japan after Nobunaga killed himself in 1582 to avoid falling into
the hands of a vassal who had betrayed him, continued to harry
the warrior-priests. In 1585 he burned Negoro-ji, in the province
of Kii (present Wakayama Prefecture), a temple of the Shingi subsect of Shingon that was a center of Buddhist military power, and
then sent an envoy to Mount Kōya, threatening to confiscate all its
holdings. Mount Kōya was spared thanks to the good offices of the
Shingon priest Mokujiki Ōgo (1536–1608), who negotiated with
Hideyoshi and dissuaded him, but the Shingon citadel was never
able to challenge secular authority again. Kokawa-dera, a Tendai
center of Buddhist military power in Kii second only to Mount
Kōya and Negoro-ji, was also burned that year. With this, the military threat of the Buddhist establishment was removed and its feudal power base greatly diminished.

Hideyoshi applied economic pressure, interfering in the affairs
of temple landholdings in conjunction with military assaults. This
considerably weakened the great temples, finally bringing them
under his control. Having accomplished this, he adopted a concil-
iatory approach when it served his interest. He lifted his ban on
the Nichiren sect and aided the restoration of Hongan-ji, the
temples of Mount Hiei and Mount Kōya, and Kōfuku-ji. In 1585
he began construction of the Daibutsu-den (Great Buddha Hall)
at the ancient Nara temple of Hōkō-ji and summoned Ōgo to
oversee the project. Ten years later he sponsored a "thousand-
priest ceremony" to dedicate the hall, inviting priests from every
sect to participate. As we will see, however, this occasion actually
provided an opportunity for further persecution of the Nichiren
sect.

The strategy of Ieyasu, Hideyoshi's successor and the first Tokugawa shōgun, was to preserve Buddhist institutions while subject-
ing them to ever stricter regulation. This policy succeeded in

bringing the Buddhist establishment completely under the control of the central feudal authority. One example of the shogunate's policy was the Temple Regulations, which affected all temples of all sects. These regulations, drafted under the supervision of the Rinzai priest Sūden (1569–1633) of Nanzen-ji, in Kyoto, established a main- and branch-temple system and prescribed the careful observance of differences in rank among temples and priests. The regulations also encouraged the pursuit of doctrinal studies by the clergy. Sūden, incidentally, had been in charge of foreign affairs during Hideyoshi's unsuccessful Korean invasions of 1592 and 1597, and later served Ieyasu in the same capacity. The Tendai priest Tenkai (d. 1643) also played an active role in affairs of state.

The establishment of main and branch temples was a convenient means of bringing the Buddhist establishment into conformity with the pattern of feudal control, and the encouragement of scholasticism was intended to discourage priests from looking beyond the walls of the cloister. As a result, temples constructed facilities for study, and priests began to analyze their sects' doctrines in minute detail. The emphasis on doctrine led to the formalization of teachings, and important religious issues degenerated into petty debate. Those who proffered new teachings or innovative interpretations were tried and punished by the shogunate. In 1635 an Office of Temples and Shrines was instituted to oversee the business and legal affairs of all religious institutions and to investigate and punish irregularities.

Another way in which the Tokugawa shogunate regulated the Buddhist establishment was through the creation of the parish, or *danka,* system. Actually, the parish system originated in the persecution of Christianity. Nobunaga had encouraged Christianity for a time, largely to irk his Buddhist rivals. But from the time of Hideyoshi onward the authorities persecuted Christianity, and after the Shimabara Uprising of 1637, a Christian-led peasant uprising in the predominantly Christian domain of Shimabara (in present Nagasaki Prefecture), the religion was proscribed. To eradicate Christianity, in 1639 the authorities declared a policy of national seclusion, permitting few foreigners to enter and no Japanese to leave the country, and the following year instituted the office of religious inquisitor. Every Japanese was required to register as the parishioner of a temple. On occasions such as marriage, travel, employment, or change of residence, a certificate from the temple was required testifying that the person was not a Christian but a bona fide Buddhist parishioner.

Though Buddhist institutions were robbed of much of their power and prestige by the shogunate, at the same time, through the religious inquisition policy and the parish system in particular, they were protected and provided with means of support. As long as they cooperated with the shogunate's policies, their security was guaranteed. Of course, the system also invited corruption, and this was to serve as a rallying point for the anti-Buddhist movement that arose in the seventeenth century. This movement was spearheaded by eminent Confucian, Shintō, and Kokugaku (National Learning) scholars, including Nakae Tōju (1608–48), Kumazawa Banzan (1619–91), Yamaga Sokō (1622–85), Itō Jinsai (1627–1705), Ogyū Sorai (1666–1728), Motoori Norinaga (1730–1801), and Hirata Atsutane (1776–1843). A few leaders of the movement had originally belonged to the Buddhist clergy: Fujiwara Seika (1561–1619), Hayashi Razan (1583–1657), and Yamazaki Ansai (1619–82), all Neo-Confucian scholars, had been Rinzai priests.

The attack on Buddhism covered many fronts: the institution of the clergy; Buddhism's rejection of the world; its theories of transmigration, karmic retribution, and hell and paradise; its concept of sin; and the practice of cremation. In fact, the opponents of Buddhism often criticized the universal and transcendental focus of Buddhism from the standpoint of the feudalistic and secular moral concepts of Confucianism, Shintō, and Kokugaku or a simplistic, emotionalistic nationalism. Though it would not have been difficult for the Buddhists to triumph in debates conducted on this level, they would have done well to take to heart their opponents' specific charges of abuse and corruption.

The specific charges were as follows. Despite the poverty of the people, Buddhist institutions continued to spend huge sums on the construction of temple buildings. They devoted most of their energies to sterile doctrinal quibbles, which sometimes escalated into friction between sects. They had grown greedy for the fruits of the parish system—generous gifts or cash payments on the occasions of funerals and death-anniversary services—and bestowed different ranks of posthumous Buddhist names depending upon the amount the family of the bereaved paid. If the chief priest of a temple was dissatisfied with the donation, he might delay a funeral address or refuse to issue the all-important temple-register certificate. In addition to citing these grievances of the poor, spokesmen of the anti-Buddhist movement criticized the authority and ease that the parish system afforded priests.

The Confucian scholar Itō Jinsai offered an interesting criticism of Zen priests. He said that when meditating in isolated forest groves they might seem to be awe-inspiring men of great character, but when they returned to society they grew confused and wild and were of even less worth than ordinary citizens. The reason, he explained, was that priests forgot the lessons of society while engaged in their meditations, so that when they returned to the world they were more likely than anyone else to succumb to its temptations.

Some of the critics of Buddhism anticipated modern scholarly reexamination of the religion. For example, Tominaga Nakamoto (1715–46) in *Shutsujō kōgo* [Remarks After Meditation] and Hattori Ten'yū (1724–69) in *Sekirara* [Stark Naked] challenged the orthodox belief of the time that the Mahayana Buddhist scriptures were authentic. Hirata Atsutane wrote a satirical work modeled on Nakamoto's *Shutsujō kōgo* titled *Shutsujō shōgo* [Laughter After Meditation; 1849] in which he mocked the religion in a popular, even vulgar vein. To this work he attached an appendix, "Two Sects That Are Enemies of the *Kami*," in which he criticized the Jōdo Shin and Nichiren sects as enemies of the Shintō *kami*, since they rejected worship at Shintō shrines.

According to Jōdo Shin teachings, the indigenous deities rejoiced when people were reborn in the Pure Land and made every effort to assist them. To have absolute faith in rebirth in the Pure Land and to recite the *nembutsu* were thus to follow the true will of the *kami;* but to pray at Shintō shrines for worldly benefits and to set up household Shintō altars (*kamidana*) were misguided practices. The Nichiren sect taught that Japan's deities had experienced the "divine taste" of the Buddhist Law and thus become its defenders and protectors, but that since true Buddhism did not prevail in Japan, the *kami* had abandoned the nation and returned to the celestial realm. There was no meaning in worshiping at empty shrines.

The Buddhists could and should have responded to the criticisms of the anti-Buddhists, particularly with regard to attacks from the standpoint of secular morality; but the clergy had grown so corrupt that a convincing defense was all but impossible. The anti-Buddhists frequently accused the clergy of excesses, and independent sources indicate the validity of many such charges. Jean Crasset wrote that all Buddhist priests cared for was pleasure and that they used the donations of believers to fatten their own purses. Other sources say the same. Contemporary literature and poetry describe temples as dens of lust and record the priests' pursuit of both women and men.

Around the end of the seventeenth century the finances of the warrior class became straitened as the economy moved from an agricultural to a mercantile base. The wealthy merchant class created a culture of pleasure and luxury that marked much of the rest of the Edo period. From the merchants' point of view, "priests and warriors, dogs and beasts" were one of a kind, as a popular saying of the time went. Even if some priests remained untainted by the general corruption of Buddhism, the skeptical attitude of the people made it unlikely that they could be a source of much religious inspiration.

The Buddhist establishment as a whole was corrupted and tamed by its feudal masters. But one sect of pure religious faith continued to resist authority. This was the Fuju Fuse (literally, "not receiving, not giving") subsect of Nichiren Buddhism. This subsect was held in the same disdain as Christianity—"The Christians and Fuju Fuse are the enemies of the realm, hated by the people," it was said—and, like Christianity, was proscribed for most of the Edo period. In fact, persecution continued until after the Meiji Restoration of 1868 that ended the Tokugawa shogunate. That many Fuju Fuse members were tortured and killed for their beliefs belies the general impression that Buddhism has no martyrs.

The subsect's exclusive nature is apparent from its name. "Not receiving" meant that nothing could be accepted from those not of the same belief; "not giving" meant that no alms could be given to priests of other sects (including the mainstream Nichiren sect). This uncompromising attitude can be traced directly back to Nichiren. To him, all who did not take refuge in the teachings of the Lotus Sutra, the supreme embodiment of Buddhist truth, were slanderers of the Law. And the only approach to slanderers of the Law was to refuse them alms and "break and subdue" (*shakubuku*) them. As we have seen, Nichiren's relentless drive to convert those in authority, often through rebukes to the state, called down persecution upon him and his followers.

After Nichiren's death his disciples continued the struggle. In 1398 the priests Nichinin and Nichijitsu of Myōman-ji, in Kyoto, issued a direct rebuke to the shōgun, Ashikaga Yoshimochi, for which they were arrested and tortured. After his arrival in Kyoto at the age of twenty, the priest Nisshin (1407–88) of the Nakayama branch frequently rebuked the authorities. Finally, in 1440, he was arrested on the orders of the shōgun, Ashikaga Yoshinori, and was subjected to hideous tortures by fire and water, genital mutilation, and branding, and had the tip of his tongue cut off. The climax of the government's persecution of Nisshin was the placing of a red-hot cauldron over his head. Nisshin would not relent, however, and his trials became known throughout the realm, earning him the sobriquet "Nisshin the Pot Wearer."

Two centuries later, in 1608, the priest Nichikyō (1560–1620) was scheduled to appear in a debate with Jōdo priests at Edo Castle. The night before the debate he was attacked and gravely wounded by ruffians. His disciples begged the authorities to postpone the debate, but their request was refused. Nichikyō's party lost the debate because he could not speak, and he was ordered to write an admission of defeat. He refused, arousing Ieyasu's wrath. The next year his ears and nose were cut off on the shōgun's orders, and one of his disciples was executed.

Thus, there had always been priests of the Nichiren sect who had undergone torture at the hands of the state, but with the consolidation of power under the Tokugawa regime, pressure against the sect increased and most Nichiren followers chose acquiescence. One group, however, refused to capitulate and continued to produce martyrs: the Fuju Fuse subsect.

Persecution of the Fuju Fuse subsect was catalyzed by events connected with the great "thousand-priest ceremony" that Toyotomi Hideyoshi held for the dedication of the Daibutsu-den at Hōkō-ji in 1595. Priests of all sects were invited. After some debate, the priests of the Nichiren sect decided to attend—except for Nichiō (1565–1630), the chief priest of Myōkaku-ji, in Kyoto, who adamantly refused on the grounds that when Nichiren had directed his followers not to support nonbelievers, he had also meant them to refuse to accept support. He sent a "Rebuke from the Lotus Sect" to Hideyoshi demanding that he cancel the ceremony and then, fearing that his deed would cause trouble for others in his temple, left by night to begin a life of wandering. During his travels he continued to criticize those who had agreed to participate in the ceremony. Nichiō was from the merchant class, and something of the bold entrepreneur can be seen in his actions.

So it was that the Nichiren sect was split into those who believed it acceptable to receive alms from but not give alms to nonbelievers, and those of the Fuju Fuse subsect, who held that alms could neither be received from nor given to nonbelievers. In 1599 Nichiō was called before Ieyasu to respond to charges by the Nichiren faction that had approved participation, and the following year he was banished to the island of Tsushima, off the northwestern coast of Kyūshū. He was pardoned in 1612 and returned to Kyoto, but the struggle between the two factions grew fiercer, and in 1630 he was sentenced once more to exile on Tsushima. He died before the sentence could be carried out, however, so his remains were exiled in his stead. Six priests were exiled along with Nichiō's ashes.

The Fuju Fuse subsect continued to strengthen, finally provoking the shogunate to harsh measures: Fuju Fuse temples were required to provide receipts for their temples, grounds, and even water and roads, for the government claimed that all these belonged to the state. Unless the temples provided them—thus acknowledging that they were receiving from nonbelievers—the government would no longer permit them to issue certificates to parishioners as required by the parish system and would exile their priests. If Fuju Fuse parishioners could no longer receive certificates from their temples, they became in effect outlaws, excluded from society. Some Fuju Fuse priests left their temples to preach in the streets, but the shogunate prohibited that, as well.

In response to these measures, most Fuju Fuse priests went underground. Many followers changed their registration to less intransigent branches of the Nichiren sect or even to other sects, while secretly clinging to their Fuju Fuse beliefs. But the most fervent Fuju Fuse members adopted a more radical approach, embracing their outlaw status and living a life of pure faith. They held clandestine services at night, chanting the sutras and listening to sermons in storehouses or sheds with a lookout posted at the entrance. Even so, they never knew when they would be apprehended and always wore traveling clothes to be ready for escape. They hid their religious documents inside bamboo rods, under rafters, inside walls, beneath house pillars, or rolled in clay tiles buried deep in the ground. Fuju Fuse priests always carried a proclamation of their beliefs tucked in their clothing, for they were determined, if apprehended, to make a final rebuke to the government before giving up their lives.

Even with these precautions, the government managed to infiltrate the subsect with spies, and there was an unending stream of Fuju Fuse martyrs, both clerical and lay, throughout the Edo period. In one incident, a group of believers in Yatabe (in present Okayama Prefecture) was discovered in 1668. The priest Nikkan was discovered in the house of a believer and was arrested with five followers and their families—thirty-four people in all. Nikkan and his followers, all young men in their early thirties, were beheaded; the twenty-eight surviving family members, including many women and small children, were exiled. Such severe measures reveal the gravity with which the shogunate viewed any challenge to its authority. The next year Nikkan's master, Nissei, was told by the authorities that he would have to sign a receipt for his temple's water and roads. Realizing that he was not long for this world, he left his temple for a cave in Fukuda (the present city of Tsuyama, Okayama Prefecture), determined to starve himself to death. Four female believers eventually joined him, and they died together.

In addition to these well-known martyrs to the Fuju Fuse cause, many believers came to grief because of their faith. In 1691 a great search was made across the land, and sixty-three priests and eleven lay believers were exiled to the islands of Miyakejima, Ōshima, Kōzushima, Niijima, and Hachijōjima, off the Izu Peninsula. Others died in prison or took their own lives. Some islanders were converted to the Fuji Fuse faith. The graves and personal effects of the exiled priests can still be seen on the islands. Images of Shakyamuni and of Nichiren, mandalas (copies of the famous ideographic mandala created by Nichiren), and copies of the Lotus Sutra are also to be found, and many people now make group pilgrimages to the islands.

In the nineteenth century, as increasing tensions began to loosen the ties that held the feudal system together, government measures grew even more repressive. In the Tempō era (1830–44) a new search for Fuju Fuse members was mounted, and this time the subsect was effectively wiped out. After that, members and their gathering places were indicated only by code numbers, but even this failed to prevent the discovery of subsect members as persecution continued even after the demise of the shogunate.

CHAPTER TWELVE

Challenges to the Old Order

THE CONTROVERSY between Buddhism and Christianity in Japan occurred mainly during two periods: the latter half of the six-teenth century, when Christianity was first transmitted to Japan, and the latter half of the nineteenth century, when it was reintro-duced after Japan had opened its doors to the West. This contro-versy provides valuable material for the study of both Edo-period and early modern Buddhism in Japan, as well as for their compar-ison. The controversy is also important because the form it took was unique to Japan and involved basic philosophical issues.

Christianity was first brought to Japan in 1549 by the Jesuit Francis Xavier (1506–52). The Society of Jesus was founded by Ignatius of Loyola, a Spanish aristocrat, together with five others, including Xavier, in response to the threat posed to Catholicism by the Reformation. In an attempt to increase the number of Cath-olics, many of whom had been lost to Protestantism, vigorous mis-sionary efforts were extended to the East. Xavier was sent to India, and it was there that he met a Japanese youth and decided to take the Catholic teachings to Japanese shores. He landed at Kago-shima, on southern Kyūshū, in the eighth month of 1549, and dur-ing the two years or so he spent in Japan his missionary activities took him north through Kyūshū and southwestern Honshū to the Kyoto area.

Catholic missionaries soon began to arrive in quick succession and made many converts. Portuguese merchants supported the missions, and several Kyūshū daimyō, keen to reap trade benefits, welcomed the priests. Some daimyō even converted to Christianity. They received Christian names upon baptism, adopted the cross and other Christian symbols as family crests, and replaced all Buddhist temples and Shintō shrines within their domains with churches.

Ōmura Sumitada, Ōtomo Sōrin, and Arima Harunobu were among these *kirishitan* daimyō, as they were called. In 1582 they sent an embassy of teenage boys to Rome. Takayama Ukon and Konishi Yukinaga were other famous Christian daimyō of that time. Ukon was exiled to Manila in 1614, when all missionaries were expelled from Japan, and died there. Yukinaga fought on the losing side at Sekigahara in 1600 and was urged to commit ritual suicide. But since Christian doctrine forbade suicide, he surrendered instead and was executed in Kyoto.

Within forty years of the introduction of Christianity, 2 percent of the population—about 150,000 people—had been converted, there were about two hundred churches, and the religion was known from Kyūshū to the Kantō region of eastern Honshū and even farther north. One reason for the rapid spread of Christianity was, as mentioned, that some daimyō protected it, hoping to benefit from trade with the Portuguese merchants who supported the missions. Oda Nobunaga, while not a convert, is said to have tolerated the new religion as part of his plan to weaken the Buddhist establishment.

Another reason that some daimyō found it easy to accept Christianity may have been the superficial resemblance of the absolute obedience to the will of God expected of Christians to the allegiance to the feudal lord expected of vassals. The missionaries themselves stressed this parallel. Yet Japan's rulers soon began to persecute believers, and many Japanese Christians were forced to choose between their Lord in Heaven and their lord on earth. The missionaries insisted on obedience to God: "Whenever you can do so without disobeying God, serve your ruler, even at the cost of your life; but you must never obey orders that go against God's will," they preached. This commandment had a great impact on followers of the new religion and was to lead many to martyrdom.

In considering the rise and fall of Christianity in Japan, it is important to keep in mind the ordinary converts who lived in simple faith. It was the lower classes that suffered the most in the strife that swept the land during the Age of the Warring Provinces. Their spiritual needs unsatisfied by the increasing secularization of culture in general and Buddhism in particular, they felt strongly the spiritual power of Christianity and gave themselves completely to the new faith. Their devotion led many to lay down their lives during the persecutions that were to follow.

The controversy between Buddhism and Christianity began soon after Christianity reached Japan. Initially the Christians took the initiative, for they aimed to cut into Buddhism's base of support among the people. But when the persecutions began, the Buddhists took the offensive, though because they were trying to ingratiate themselves with the secular authorities their response to the Christian challenge fell short of its initial high tone, when purely doctrinal differences had been the main concern.

The first debates were between Christian missionaries and priests of the Nichiren and Zen sects. To begin with, the Christians were highly impressed with believers in the Lotus Sutra: "The followers of the Lotus sect in Kyoto are deeper thinkers than those of any other sect," states one contemporary Christian source. As the missionaries came to feel more threatened by their adversaries, however, their evaluation changed: "The priests of the Lotus sect hate us and God most." "The priests who worship Shakyamuni and call themselves [followers of] the Lotus sect are the greatest enemies of the Gospel."

Debates between Buddhists and Christians are described in many sources: the reports of the missionary activities of the Society of Jesus in Japan regularly dispatched to Rome, missionaries' letters, and such books as Luis Frois's *História de Japam* [History of Japan] and Jean Crasset's history of Christianity in Japan. Frois participated in many debates during his travels around the country and reported on them in letters to the headquarters of the Society of Jesus. He also wrote the reports of Jesuit activities in Japan mentioned above.

The central issues of the early debates were the existence of a Creator God and the immortality of the soul. These are in fact two of the essential differences between Buddhism and Christianity. The Buddhists asked why, if God created the world, he allowed evil to exist, and maintained that the Christian doctrine of eternal damnation showed a lack of compassion in the Christian God. They contrasted this with the boundless compassion of the Buddha and the Buddhist teaching that even those in hell will eventually achieve enlightenment. The Christians in turn asserted that since the Buddha was a mortal, not an absolute deity, he had no power to save human beings. They also criticized Buddhism for monism, since it regarded good and evil as complementary opposites that were essentially empty. Although Japanese Buddhism had been infiltrated by a mystical belief in spirits, when debating Christians the Buddhists reverted to Buddhism's more radical position of denying the dualism of body and spirit and the immortality of the soul. Many finer points of doctrine and belief were also debated. What is particularly worthy of note is how accurately the essential features of each religion were identified and how central these were to the arguments. This was the reason for the high intellectual level of the early controversy.

The Christian missionaries praised Nobunaga's burning of the temple buildings of Enryaku-ji, on Mount Hiei, in 1571 as the execution of God's will. Frois wrote to the regional superior in India: "Omnipotent and supremely good God must be praised for opening the way for the propagation of the holy teachings by destroying our rivals in this fashion." But by the time of the ascendance of Hideyoshi the Buddhist establishment was securely under the control of the state and there was no longer any need to encourage Christianity as a check to Buddhist ambitions. Hideyoshi adopted a harsh policy toward the new religion and offered his support and protection to Buddhism instead. He was especially alarmed by the aggressive missionary activities of the newly arrived Franciscan priests. The first expulsion of missionaries took place upon his orders in 1587. Ten years later he had twenty-six Christians, including both foreign priests and Japanese believers—the so-called Twenty-six Martyrs—crucified in Nagasaki, western Kyūshū.

Ieyasu, concerned with the success of trade, refrained from harsh persecution of Christianity, and the religion recovered somewhat during his rule. But by the time of his successors as shōgun, first Hidetada (1579–1632) and then Iemitsu (1604–51), the shogunate had had a chance to consolidate its control of the nation and was prepared to take a firmer stance. It was around that time, too, that the Protestant Dutch, latecomers to the scramble for trade concessions, began to advise the shogunate that the Spanish and Portuguese were using Catholicism as a shield for territorial designs on Japan. Far-reaching persecution of Christianity began.

In 1612 Christianity was prohibited in all domains under direct Tokugawa control and among direct Tokugawa vassals. Two years later, as noted, all Christian missionaries were expelled. The daimyō Takayama Ukon and other converts were exiled, and churches were torn down. In 1629 the third shōgun, Iemitsu, instituted the infamous *fumi-e* test of loyalty, which required people suspected of being Christians to step on (*fumi*) a Christian image (*e*). If they refused, they were arrested and punished. The importation of Christian books was prohibited in 1630, neighborhood groups (*gonin-gumi*) were strengthened and ordered to make secret reports of any Christians under their jurisdiction in 1637, and in the same year the massacre at Shimabara took place. Finally, in 1639, Japan was closed to the outside world, and the next year anti-Christian inquisitors were appointed. Some Christians chose to conform to the letter of the law while secretly practicing their beliefs; they were known as "hidden Christians" (*kakure kirishitan*). But they, too, were regularly exposed and prosecuted, though hidden-Christian communities managed to survive in isolated areas. A group of about thirty thousand such believers exists to this day on northern Kyūshū and nearby islands.

The feudal ethic that was based on the values of the warrior class was emphasized throughout the Edo period, but by the end

of the seventeenth century the warriors were growing more impoverished as the merchant class became wealthier with the expansion of commerce. The warriors continued to adhere to the
old values, which they considered superior to those of the merchants, but the merchants were fast producing their own values,
which transcended the rigid class barriers decreed by the shogunate. The warriors looked down on the merchants' pursuit of profit
and congratulated themselves on their noble dedication to duty.
But to the merchants, the life of the warrior amounted to nothing
more than putting a good face on a bad situation.

The characters that appear in the works of such representative
writers of merchant culture as Ihara Saikaku (1642–93) and Chikamatsu Monzaemon (1653–1724) frequently reflect the pride of the
merchants and their sense of equality with the warriors. Saikaku
was born into a merchant family in Osaka, and his novels concern
the lives and loves of townspeople. The playwright Chikamatsu
Monzaemon was the second son in a warrior family, but many of
his works, written for the Kabuki and puppet theaters, are tragic
tales of love among the merchant class of Osaka. The renowned
astronomer Nishikawa Joken (1648–1724) wrote bluntly of his high
birth: "It was a bother to be born into a warrior family: always
fearfully serving the lord, never a moment's peace of mind. Not
being so concerned with reputation and all sorts of silly displays,
the ordinary townsman has a lot more fun."

The merchants believed in following their feelings rather than
observing stiff customs as the warrior class did even in intimate
matters. They considered the love of husband and wife important
but also recognized remarriage and even romantic love. The respect for natural feelings that characterized the merchant class influenced the larger culture.

The haiku poems of Matsuo Bashō (1644–94) are an example.
The haiku format—three lines, of five, seven, and five syllables—
existed before Bashō's time as a comic element in the complex
linked-verse form called *renga,* but Bashō made the haiku into a
high art form in its own right. Born into a warrior family, he relin-
quished his status and traveled all over Japan, living among towns-

people and peasants. In fact he died on the road. In his poems he created a realm that melded nature and human feelings. Though firmly wedded to the ordinary and near at hand, his poems are richly evocative and refined. The influence of merchant culture was also felt in the performing arts of Kabuki and the puppet theater, in music, and in woodblock prints and other fine arts, resulting in works of the highest aesthetic quality.

In the area of philosophy, the Ancient Learning (*kogaku*) movement arose to challenge the Neo-Confucian orthodoxy that served as a tool of the state. The Ancient Learning scholars studied the writings of the ancient Confucian sages and tried to apply them to daily life. The main figures in this movement were two masterless warriors of Edo, Yamaga Sokō and Ogyū Sorai, and Itō Jinsai, who was from a merchant family in Kyoto.

In his *Seikyō yōroku* [Essentials of the Sacred Teachings], Sokō rejected the doctrines of the Neo-Confucians Chu Hsi and Wang Yang-ming. He maintained that the "sacred teachings" taught ethics and rejected the idea that the bonds of loyalty between subject and lord transcended history or were absolute. He also emphasized the importance of studying history, the human heart, and customs. Sokō was temporarily banished from Edo for his beliefs. Jinsai taught that ethics was a matter of individual determination. Like Sokō, he rejected the Chu Hsi belief in the "heavenly mandate" of rulers, propounding a humanistic and pragmatic philosophy. Sorai, who was influenced by Jinsai, maintained that ethics was a matter not of religion but of individual conscience and that the precepts handed down by great religious leaders and the laws enacted by rulers were not absolute but had to change with the times.

The humanism of the Ancient Learning movement influenced the study of classical Japanese literature. The Kokugaku, or National Learning, movement was founded by the Shingon priest Keichū (1640–1701) and others who studied the ancient *Man'yōshū* poetry anthology. It continued to develop under the aegis of such scholars as Kada no Azumamaro (1669–1736) and Kamo no Mabuchi (1697–1769) and was brought to its culmination by the great

Motoori Norinaga. Norinaga, the son of a cotton wholesaler, practiced medicine in addition to writing. The Kokugaku scholars sought to identify the "pure" Japanese spirit that had existed before the introduction of continental civilization in the forms of Confucianism and Buddhism.

Meanwhile, the rise of the pragmatic merchant class and the emphasis on humanism led to the encouragement of various practical skills and sciences, among them economics, medicine, mathematics, astronomy, botany, physics, chemistry, and geography. The natural sciences, introduced by the Dutch, were called Rangaku, or Dutch Learning, after the Japanese pronunciation of Holland (Oranda). The philosophy called Shingaku (Heart Learning) expounded by Ishida Baigan (1685–1744) is an interesting development in this light. Shingaku taught the "way of the merchant," emphasizing complete social equality. In his *Tohi mondō* [Catechism of the Capital and the Countryside], Baigan argued that the merchant who lives off his profits is no different from the warrior who sells his rice stipend for a living, and that there is no reason to disdain either.

Education also improved and expanded with the rise of the merchant class. Many merchants' sons were educated in *terakoya*. In the language of the merchants, children were called *terako* (temple children), and *ya* means "building." These "temple schools," as they are often called in English, were originally in temples, but later they were established in ordinary homes in towns and cities, and the boys were taught by masterless warriors and merchants, as well as Buddhist and Shintō priests. This wide base of elementary education was to serve Japan well in its efforts to modernize in the second half of the nineteenth century.

The culture of the merchants flowered again in the first decades of the nineteenth century but became more self-indulgent and even escapist. One reason is that though the merchants held the purse strings, power was still firmly in the grip of the warriors, so it was impossible for merchants to participate fully in society. The only outlet for their energies was conspicuous consumption. That the merchant culture was above all a consumer culture distinguishes it from the capitalist European culture of the same period. The industrial revolution in Europe harnessed the power of the working class, which eventually overturned the old feudal order and built a new social order. The Japanese masses never reached the point of changing the status quo, and though the merchant culture reached great heights in many ways, the feudal nature of society was preserved. Confucianism, Kokugaku, Buddhism, and other systems of thought were all expounded from above for the edification of the people. The merchants could rebel only by refusing to invest in the shogunate's future and by spending their earnings on pleasure.

Despite the general spiritual impoverishment of the Buddhist establishment, the Edo period did produce some priests of great distinction and learning. Three Rinzai priests deserve special mention. Takuan Sōhō (1573–1645) opposed the Temple Regulations and was once exiled for that stance, though later he became a valued adviser to the shōgun Iemitsu. His *Tōkai yawa* [Eastern Sea Night Talks] advocates diligence and virtue and criticizes luxury. Takuan is also famous as the spiritual instructor of the master swordsman Yagyū Munenori. Bankei Yōtaku (1622–93) expounded what he called "easy Zen" or "practical Zen." He taught that everyone has an "unborn and undying buddha-mind" and called this philosophy "unborn Zen." His straightforward and down-to-earth way of speaking won him many followers. Hakuin Ekaku (1685–1768) was in some ways similar to Bankei. Regarded as the reviver of the Rinzai sect, he left many collections of sermons written in the phonetic *hiragana* syllabary to make them accessible to a wide readership.

The Sōtō sect of Zen produced Suzuki Shōsan (1579–1655), another prolific writer. He taught that secular laws are consistent with Buddhist truths and that work is a form of Buddhist practice, emphasizing practical virtues and the work ethic. Ryōkan (1758–1831), another remarkable Sōtō priest, excelled in poetry, was well known for his eccentricities, and had great compassion for all living beings.

The Ōbaku sect of Ch'an Buddhism originally was introduced

from China in 1654 by a mission led by Yin-yüan Lung-chi (1592–1673), the head of the sect. Ōbaku is actually a subsect of Rinzai, but its teachings include elements of Pure Land Buddhism, as well. Tetsugen Dōkō (1630–82) was a famous disciple of Yin-yüan. The Tendai priest Tenkai had published the complete Buddhist canon with the support of the shogunate, but Tetsugen accomplished the same feat with no official support, completing the task in 1681. Active in assisting victims of earthquakes and other natural disasters, he was revered by the people. It was their support that enabled him to raise the funds needed to publish the canon.

Jiun Onkō (also known as Jiun Sonja; 1718–1804) was an eminent Shingon priest who strove to restore the Buddhist precepts and regulations known as the *vinaya*. He also studied the Sanskrit and Siddham scripts and composed a thousand-volume study of Sanskrit that remains a masterpiece. He, too, wrote sermons in *hiragana* to reach a wide readership.

The Tendai priests Jizan Myōryū (1637–90) and Reikū Kōken (1652–1739) sought to reform their sect, emphasizing the *vinaya*. Another priest concerned with the *vinaya* was Gensei (also called Nissei; 1623–68) of the Nichiren sect. The precepts that he instituted were later known as the Sōzan *Vinaya* or the Lotus *Vinaya*. He was also an accomplished poet and left several poetry collections. Hōtan (1659–1738) of the Kegon school and Fujaku Tokumon (1707–81) of the Seizan subsect of the Jōdo sect did much to improve the fortunes of their sects. Fujaku, well versed in the teachings of all Japanese Buddhist sects, was in many ways the precursor of modern Buddhist scholars in Japan.

There were many other pious priests and learned scholars during the Edo period. But all of them clung to the ethics of feudalism, however closely they worked with the people. They taught that people should work to perfect themselves within the prescribed limits of their social status. Such was the position of the Buddhist establishment; Buddhist reform movements had to wait until the modern period, which began with the collapse of the shogunate and the Meiji Restoration of 1868.

CHAPTER THIRTEEN

Religious Reform Movements

I N 1868 THE FEUDALISTIC, isolationist Tokugawa regime came to an end as a new government headed by the young Emperor Meiji was established and Japan entered the company of modern nation-states. Actually, the first breezes of modernization had wafted through Japan before the Meiji Restoration, and there had been popular resistance to the feudalistic policies of the shogunate in the form of peasant uprisings (*ikki*) and *yo naoshi* (world renewal) movements involving not only peasants but also the lower strata of urban society.

Unlike townspeople, who enjoyed relative material comfort despite their low status in the official class system, peasants suffered from both economic and social oppression. The peasant uprisings were an inevitable result of the institutionalized oppression of the agricultural class that was part and parcel of shogunate policy. In the mid-eighteenth century the peasant class found an articulate spokesman in Andō Shōeki (1703?–62), who was born in a farm village in the poor Tōhoku region of northeastern Honshū. In his writings he advocated a unique "peasant philosophy," claiming that the warriors, who lived off the annual rice levies received from the peasants, were criminals "greedy for food but unwilling to work." In general, he criticized warriors as parasites and praised peasants because they were engaged in productive labor.

Shōeki condemned the class system of feudal society and advocated egalitarianism; in that regard he is rightly recognized as a herald of modern ideas. On the other hand, he espoused a "natural philosophy" that sought to restore his vision of ancient ways. He was opposed to trade and held that society should be exclusively agricultural. Because this position was too far removed from the reality of Edo-period Japan, it failed to contribute in a tangible way to reform of feudal society or improvement of peasants' lives.

Lack of realism was also a flaw of another reformist group, the *myōkōnin* (literally, "wonderfully good ones"), followers of the Jōdo Shin sect who were devout practitioners of the *nembutsu*. Though merchants, warriors, and priests were to be found among their ranks, most *myōkōnin* were peasants. Their faith was a simple one, but they grasped the essential truths of their religion and thus had a great effect on those around them. Nevertheless, their conviction that everything should be left to Amida often resulted in acquiescence to authority. There were of course cases in which conflict between Jōdo Shin followers and the authorities arose and the former became targets of official persecution. This was especially likely when a conflict was felt to exist between the secular duty of loyalty to one's lord and reverence for Amida. Yet on more than one occasion when groups of peasants rose in rebellion, *myōkōnin* refused to participate and even admonished the rebels.

As mentioned earlier, several major uprisings occurred in the fifteenth century when Rennyo was the chief abbot of Hongan-ji, whose followers joined local peasants in revolt. But as the Jōdo Shin organization was absorbed into the feudal structure and became part of the establishment, resistance gave way to compliance. The *myōkōnin* exemplify this "adjustment" to the feudal system and, from the point of view of the *yo naoshi* movements of the late Edo period, must be regarded as part of the establishment. Moreover, the Jōdo Shin temple Nishi Hongan-ji, in Kyoto, strove to spread the Pure Land teachings to the lowest level of Japanese society, the outcast population, which specialized in occupations considered unclean by Buddhists, such as those involving the handling of carcasses. The outcasts were taught that because of their lowly and persecuted status they were the special objects of Amida's compassion and would enjoy rebirth in Amida's Pure Land after death. Though this may have consoled them, it also encouraged them to accept their status and even obstructed efforts to liberate them from it.

Nevertheless, the peasants' lot was so hard that the limit of endurance was often breached. During the Edo period there were more than sixteen hundred peasant uprisings. Their frequency rose dramatically around the mid-eighteenth century, when the strains inherent in the feudal system were becoming apparent. Uprisings among the lower strata of townspeople began to occur with increasing frequency around the same time. In 1786 alone there were fifteen peasant uprisings nationwide. The following year riots broke out in Osaka and spread to cities throughout the realm. Rioting was especially violent in Edo, the seat of the shogunate.

In the 1830s another rash of rebellions in both cities and the countryside was triggered by poor harvests, famines, and high rice prices. The wealth and land of the privileged were seized in an attempt to right economic wrongs and establish greater equality. The earlier peasant revolts, focused on such issues as taxes, had thus evolved into reform movements with larger purposes. One of the best-known revolts of that decade was led by Ōshio Heihachirō (1793–1837). The son of a constable in Osaka, he followed his father in that calling. He was greatly influenced by Confucian teachings and founded a school called the Senshin-dō to propagate his beliefs. Heihachirō was shocked and moved by the sufferings of the people during the great famine of 1836, and in the second month of the following year he led a rebellion in Osaka. He declared that even the lowliest had "descended from Heaven," and his respect for their human dignity attracted many people to his cause. The uprising was quickly quashed, however, and Heihachirō and his son took their own lives. But before that sad conclusion, his cause had spread throughout the realm and was assured great and lasting influence.

Uprisings reached a third peak in 1866, when the shogunate's administrative outposts and moneylenders were attacked and registers of deeds and loan records were burned. These uprisings gradually escalated into rebellion against the shogunate itself and hastened its downfall. The central government and various daimyō attempted reforms to appease the people, but they were unable to stem the tide of the times. Antishogunate forces among the warriors and the court establishment harnessed popular resistance to the government, and the shogunate, denied its supply of peasant soldiers through massive desertions, could no longer resist its opponents.

Yo naoshi sentiment sometimes took the form of religious movements, such as the *Ee ja nai ka* (Why not?) movement of 1867, which grew out of the popular practice of mass pilgrimages. Because of the restrictions of feudal life, which included, for the common people, not only the ties of family and profession but also a ban on unauthorized travel, most people were not free to make pilgrimages to temples and shrines whenever they wished. As a result, the practice of *okage mairi* (thanksgiving pilgrimage) or *nuke mairi* (surreptitious pilgrimage) to Ise Grand Shrine grew up. People would simply slip away, without the permission of family or employer, and set out on pilgrimage. The term *okage mairi* is said to derive from the fact that pilgrims received donations of food and lodging from people along the way.

Pilgrimages to Ise Grand Shrine became popular festive occasions in the Muromachi period. By the seventeenth century they had evolved into mass pilgrimages, which spread nationwide and grew in scale in the eighteenth century. From time to time, rumors that talismans from Ise Grand Shrine had fallen from heaven would spark pilgrimages of hundreds of thousands, or even millions, of worshipers. It is recorded that in 1830 the number of *okage mairi* pilgrims totaled 4,862,088. *Okage mairi* offered the common people a temporary release from the strictures of feudal society and can be regarded as a form of passive popular resistance to the Tokugawa regime.

Eventually the practice of *okage mairi* generated a *yo naoshi* movement in the form of the *Ee ja nai ka* craze in the autumn and winter of 1867. The *Ee ja nai ka* outburst began in the Kyoto-Osaka area, touched off by rumors late in the eighth month of that year that talismans from Ise Grand Shrine were falling from heaven in the Nagoya area. The rumors inspired huge crowds to dance while chanting "Ee ja nai ka." By the tenth month the frenzy had spread almost nationwide. This occurred just as the shogunate was on the verge of relinquishing power to the imperial supporters, and there is evidence that antishogunate forces encouraged the *Ee ja nai ka* movement for their own purposes.

What was the *Ee ja nai ka* movement? In high hopes of "world renewal," people of all classes gathered and danced through the streets, chanting "Ee ja nai ka" while accompanying themselves on flute, drum, and the three-stringed banjolike samisen. They dressed in colorful and outrageous costumes, men donning women's clothes and women men's, and danced from morning to night. They also broke into the homes of wealthy landlords and merchants, demanding food and drink and appropriating their hosts' valuables with the refrain "I'll take this—why not?" When tired, they slept wherever they dropped, only to rejoin the dancing when they awoke.

The frustrations of the oppressed common people found a release in the form of religious frenzy in *okage mairi* and, especially, the *Ee ja nai ka* movement. This movement created the illusion of liberation and as a result diverted energy from social reform, and the excitement and loss of self-control that accompanied religious frenzy sometimes resulted in immoral behavior. The crowds were without leaders or an organizational framework. As spontaneous gatherings driven by mass psychology, they lacked unity and purpose. Flawed and limited though the *Ee ja nai ka* movement was, however, through it the masses, expressing their keen desire for a new and better world as they danced and chanted through the streets, hastened the fall of the old regime.

Some highly organized new religious movements also took form in the late Edo period and the early years of the Meiji era (1868–1912). Fuji *kō*, a precursor of these, constitutes a prominent example of the many *kō*, voluntary assemblies or guilds, usually with a religious focus, that were formed in premodern times. The *kō* became a popular form of religious organization in the medieval period. *Kō* might be centered on faith in a bodhisattva, such as Jizō *kō* (devoted to the bodhisattva known in Sanskrit as Kshitigarbha) or Kannon *kō* (devoted to Avalokiteshvara); a great Buddhist teacher, such as Daishi *kō*, devoted to Kōbō Daishi (Kūkai); a Buddhist practice, such as *nembutsu kō;* a folk deity, such as Kōshin *kō;* a Shintō shrine, such as Ise *kō;* or a sacred mountain, such as Fuji *kō*. In the Edo period, *kō* serving social and professional functions were also founded, and when such functions were combined with a shared religious purpose, the *kō* became powerful organizations that occasionally offered strong resistance to the shogunate.

Mountain worship seems to have existed in Japan since very early times. In the medieval period it became linked with the teachings and practices of esoteric Buddhism and developed, through the influence of the Shingon and Tendai sects, into the unique blend of Shintō and esoteric Buddhism known as Shugendō. Certain mountains in each region of Japan had long been held sacred, and there Shugendō practitioners, known as *yamabushi* (mountain ascetics), pursued their ascetic and mystical practices. Eventually *yamabushi* took up residence in farming villages and cities, as well, and *kō* formed around them. The *kō* for worship of Mount Fuji and those for worship of Mount Ontake were among the most vigorous of these organizations.

Hasegawa Kakugyō (reputed to have lived 1541–1646) provided the Fuji *kō* with a doctrinal and structural base, after which they coalesced into a unified cult. In the mid-Edo period two leaders further contributed to the development of Fuji *kō*, Jikigyō Miroku (1671–1733) and Murakami Kōsei (1682–1759). Jikigyō Miroku was the religious name of Itō Ihei, an oil merchant. Miroku (though written with different ideograms) is the Japanese pronunciation of Maitreya, the future buddha, who will eventually appear in the world to save all sentient beings.

By incorporating elements of the Maitreya cult, Jikigyō Miroku gave Fuji *kō* a *yo naoshi* coloring and provided a doctrinal rationale for what had been a mountain cult centered on magical prayers and practices. In this way he created a strong organization unified by firm spiritual ties. By the 1830s the Fuji *kō* had become so popular in Edo that they were known as the "eight hundred eight *kō* of Edo" and claimed seventy thousand followers. Miniature Mount Fujis were built throughout Edo and attracted crowds of worshipers. Fuji *kō* also provided the nucleus for professional guilds. Around that time Kotani Sanshi (also known as Rokugyō Sanshi; 1765–1841) of the Miroku branch of Fuji *kō* eliminated all Buddhist elements in an attempt to make it a purely Shintō cult. Fujidō (Unified Path) was the name he gave to his version of the cult, which emphasized the ethical principles of service and gratitude.

The shogunate began to feel threatened by Fuji *kō* as it grew in popularity, and in 1849 both Fuji *kō* and Fujidō were prohibited. Magical practices were the ostensible reason for the ban, but in fact the authorities were concerned that these organizations would serve as focal points for popular dissatisfaction. That is exactly what happened when the Fujidō leader Shibata Shōgyō (1809–90) joined forces with those who wished to restore the emperor to power. Shōgyō had been a student of Kokugaku before joining Fujidō and devoting himself to proselytization. After the Meiji Restoration Fujidō changed its name to Jikkōkyō and another group, known as Maruyamakyō, split off from Fuji *kō*, but most Fuji *kō* members regrouped under the name Fusōkyō (Fusō is an archaic name for Japan; *kyō*, meaning "teaching," indicates a religious organization).

The government under which Japan's modernization commenced restored imperial rule. Anachronistic though that may seem, history offers abundant examples of the leaders of a new age looking to the ancient past for a model for the new order. In Japan, when the warriors who established the Kamakura shogunate sought a model for the new order, they studied precedents from ancient times, which they compiled in such collections as *Kojidan* [Stories About the Past], *Zoku kojidan* [Further Stories About the Past], and *Kokon chomon shū* [Fables Old and New]. Many Buddhists harked back to the time of Prince Shōtoku, whom they revered as having established the faith in Japan.

Nevertheless, the restoration of imperial rule as the vehicle of

modernization was problematic, because it led to absolute monarchy and a nationalism centered on the emperor. There are many
conflicting viewpoints even today as to why the Restoration took
that course. The kindest interpretation is that the threatening
presence of Western nations required the creation of a strong state,
while domestically, restoration of the emperor was a convenient
rallying point for the antishogunate forces. Some scholars have
also suggested that Japan had no tradition of absolute monarchy
and that it resulted from the introduction of Western thought.
Whatever interpretation we favor, the fact is that the Restoration
led to absolute monarchy, and a power structure with the emperor
at the apex evolved. A new elite came to power, and the people's
hopes for liberation were disappointed.

With the establishment of a nation-state under the emperor,
Shintō was made the state religion, and other religions were sub-
ordinated to it. This created pressure for modernization of the religious movements of the eighteenth and nineteenth centuries, as
well as the established Buddhist sects. Let us look first at the Buddhist establishment.

An imperial decree ordering the separation of Buddhism and
Shintō was issued in March 1868, the first year of the Meiji era.
The Buddhist titles that Shintō deities had borne for centuries
were revoked, and all Buddhist paraphernalia was removed from
Shintō shrines. Buddhist priests affiliated with Shintō shrines were
laicized or reassigned to Buddhist temples. Anti-Buddhist sentiment
arose, and in many parts of the country Buddhist temples, images,
and altar fittings were vandalized or burned.

Some Buddhists resisted this trend vigorously, calling for "uprisings to protect the Dharma" (*gohō ikki*), but many thoughtful clerics
reflected that they were being presented with an opportunity to
reform their religion and end its longstanding abuses. The Shingon priest Watanabe Unshō (1827–1909) and the Jōdo priest
Fukuda Gyōkai (1809–88), for example, called for reform of Buddhist institutions and clergy. But even progressive priests like these
defended Buddhism from the point of view of the unity of Shintō,
Confucianism, and Buddhism. They remained conservative in their

view of Christianity and approved of its persecution, based as this was on the perception of Japan as an imperial state.

After separating Buddhism and Shintō, the government pressed on with attempts to unify the nation by means of Shintō. In 1869 the government established an Office of Propaganda (Senkyōshi), and the following year it issued a proclamation advocating the propagation of the "Great Teaching" (Taikyō), that is, Shintō. But the limits of the attempt to popularize Shintō in this way soon became clear, and in 1872 a Ministry of Religion (Kyōbushō) was established that included both Shintō and Buddhist priests. These clerical bureaucrats were enjoined to promulgate the "three articles of instruction": respect for the *kami* and love of the nation, the principle of heaven and the path of humankind, and reverence for the emperor and obedience to his reign. Shintō was given precedence, but Buddhism was invoked as an ally in the cause of establishing imperial authority through policies that included the persecution of Christianity.

The Buddhist establishment, so recently the victim of the anti-Buddhist movement, decided to cooperate with the government in an attempt to recover its vigor and influence. In 1872 a coalition of Buddhist sects applied to the government for the establishment of an Office of Religion (Daikyō-in) for the training of clergy. This was approved the same year, but even within the Office of Religion Shintō enjoyed precedence, and the *kami* and buddhas continued in their strange embrace.

Also in 1872, the Buddhist reformer Shimaji Mokurai (1838–1911), a Jōdo Shin priest of Nishi Hongan-ji, toured Europe, where his observations led him to write a report to the government in December 1872 stating that the "three articles of instruction" represented an irrational confusion of government and religion. On returning to Japan he led a movement of the four branches of Jōdo Shin to withdraw from the Office of Religion. Permission was granted in January 1875, and in May that year the Office of Religion was abolished.

The campaign to eliminate the Office of Religion was the first step in the movement for the separation of religion and state and for freedom of religion, a movement that was led by Buddhist priests who had traveled abroad and come into contact with Western thought and that was supported by liberal thinkers. There were, then, some within the Buddhist establishment who made efforts to modernize their religion by embracing currents of Western thought.

The greatest fruits of the modernization of Buddhism were in the field of Buddhist studies. Beginning in 1868 a steady stream of Buddhists traveled to Europe to study. There they came into contact with Western ideas and learned modern research methods, which they took back to Japan. By the 1890s great strides had been made in Buddhist studies in Japan. The major focus of interest was textual studies, especially the study of texts written in the two ancient Indian canonical languages, Sanskrit and Pali, which had been largely unknown or ignored in Japan. Many widely accepted ideas about Japanese Buddhism were overturned by this research. The value of the key doctrines of various sects was called into question; some scholars even maintained that Mahayana Buddhism was not true Buddhism and that Japanese Buddhists should abandon it and take refuge instead in "early Buddhism," or "fundamental Buddhism." The Jōdo Shin priest Murakami Senshō (1851–1929) wrote an influential work titled *Bukkyō tōitsu ron* [The Unity of Buddhism] that criticized sectarian prejudices and explored the revolutionary idea of a unified Buddhism.

The Buddhist sects also began to modernize institutionally. In the 1890s they started establishing seminaries and universities based on European models. Sectarian organization was also modernized, and a new emphasis was placed on propagation, social welfare activities, and overseas missionary activities.

The problem of the evolution of Buddhist thought—the religion's most important component—remained, however. Developments in Buddhist thought in this period are open to criticism, though this is true not only of the established sects but also of new Buddhist movements and new religions.

CHAPTER FOURTEEN

Christianity and
the Buddhist Renaissance

AFTER THE SHIMABARA UPRISING of 1637, Christianity disappeared from the surface of Japanese society. A handful of "hidden Christians" managed to survive in northern Kyūshū, but eventually their day of reckoning arrived, not long after Japan was opened to the outside world.

Through most of the Edo period Japan was closed to all nations except for tightly regulated contacts with China, Korea, and the Netherlands. Dutch traders were confined to the small artificial island of Dejima, built by the Tokugawa shogunate in Nagasaki Harbor. Western missionaries who dreamed of converting Japan to Christianity managed to send a few Bibles and other Christian books into the country through Dejima. Progressive Japanese came across these books in their studies of Western learning, and some were deeply moved by the new religion they discovered therein.

In the mid-nineteenth century, as Western nations began to put ever greater pressure on Japan to open its doors, it became clear that Westerners could no longer be restricted to Dejima. In 1853 Commodore Matthew C. Perry of the United States sailed into Edo Bay with his "black ships" and presented a letter from the president requesting the opening of ports. The following year he visited Japan again and concluded a Treaty of Peace and Amity, the so-called Kanagawa Treaty, with the shogunate. This was followed by similar treaties with Britain, the Netherlands, Russia, and, in 1858,

France. These commercial treaties with Western nations signaled the end of the shogunate's policy of national seclusion. Japanese ports finally became accessible to outsiders, and Japan was opened to the West and its markets.

The end of national seclusion did not, however, mean the lifting of the ban on Christianity. The religion could be practiced and preached—but only among foreigners. The tacit agreement to permit Christian practice in the foreign community by no means extended to the Japanese, for whom the ban still held. The final Christian persecution, in Nagasaki, was yet to come.

The Western missionaries who went to Japan immediately after its opening, aware of the constraints on their activities, tried to spread Christianity indirectly. They served as doctors and nurses, opened schools of Western studies, and compiled bilingual dictionaries for use in Bible translation. But a French Catholic missionary, Prudence S. B. Girard, following the pope's directive to restore the churches of Japan, built a church in Yokohama in 1862. Two other French missionaries, Louis Auguste-Théodore Furet and Bernard T. Petitjean, built Ōura Catholic Church in Nagasaki in 1864. These conspicuous Christian activities once more brought the problem to the fore. One month after Ōura Catholic Church opened its doors, a group of "hidden Christians" from the Urakami district of Nagasaki slipped into the church with the other worshipers and declared their faith to Father Petitjean. Eventually some thirty thousand hidden Christians joined the Ōura congregation. This was heralded as the revival of Christianity in Japan.

For a time the Urakami Christians proceeded cautiously, but in 1867 it was discovered that they had bypassed the Buddhist parish system and held a private funeral for a fellow believer (under the parish system, funerals had to be held at the Buddhist temple with which the family of the deceased was affiliated). A large number were arrested, though the shogunate, fearing the wrath of the Western powers, later released them. The persecution of Christians did not end there, however; the final act was to be carried out by the Meiji government.

As part of its policy of making Shintō the state religion and also, perhaps, to demonstrate its authority, in March 1868 the government issued a proclamation prohibiting the "false teaching" of Christianity. The following month thirteen Urakami Christians were beheaded. Ignoring the protests of foreign powers, toward the end of 1869 the government decided to exterminate the Urakami Christian community once and for all, and in the first five days of 1870 over three thousand believers were arrested. The government did not order their execution this time but exiled them, dispersing them among twenty-one domains scattered across the nation. The local authorities, to curry favor with the central government, applied extremely cruel tortures to the exiles, and many died.

In February 1873 the government came to the realization that the ban on Christianity was an obstacle to smooth relations with the West and revoked it. The next month the surviving Urakami Christians were allowed to return home, but more than a thousand had either died or "disappeared." Their martyrdom, the consequence of the reintroduction of Christianity to Japan, was the last major persecution. After the ban was lifted, Christianity was freely practiced and preached. The activity of Protestant missionaries was especially noticeable. The Americans John Liggins and Channing Moore Williams, who arrived in Japan in 1859, are generally regarded as the first Protestant missionaries in Japan, though this is because earlier Protestant missionaries, such as James Curtis Hepburn, had not openly preached their religion.

Meanwhile, from the late 1880s onward a reaction against the westernization of Japan began to grow. Academic societies and other groups promoting Japanese nationalism sprang up, and Christianity again came under attack as a symbol of the West. Japanese Buddhists, as pointed out in chapter 13, had come into contact with modern Western thought and as a result advocated freedom of religion. But when the ban on Christianity was lifted and, backed by the prestige of "advanced" Western civilization, Christianity began making inroads among the Japanese once again, Buddhist leaders grew apprehensive. It was at this time that the nationalistic anti-Christian movement arose.

Seeing an opportunity to advance their own cause, many Buddhists affiliated themselves with the nationalists and launched a movement to promote and protect Buddhism under the rubric of "revering the emperor and protecting the nation." The Great Alliance to Revere the Emperor and Serve the Buddha (Sonnō Hōbutsu Daidōdan), founded in 1889 by Ōuchi Seiran (1845–1918), a priest of the Hongan-ji subsect of the Jōdo Shin sect, was representative of this new Buddhist activity. Ironically, Shimaji Mokurai, who had advocated freedom of religion, cooperated with this organization and went so far as to declare that the emperor and Christianity could not coexist.

The intellectual assault on Christianity was typified by Inoue Enryō (1858–1919). The first criticism of Christianity in the Meiji era was offered by Ugai Tetsujō (1814–91) of the Jōdo sect. At the height of the anti-Buddhist movement he wrote two tracts that defended Buddhism by attacking Christianity: *Shōya ron* [Laughing at Christianity] and *Buppō fukaseki ron* [The Buddhist Law Is Irrefutable]. Enryō inherited his mantle and carried the intellectual criticism of Christianity to a new height.

Brought up in a temple of the Ōtani subsect of the Jōdo Shin sect, Inoue Enryō studied philosophy at Tokyo Imperial University and wrote over 120 works. In 1887 he founded the Tetsugakukan (Institute of Philosophy), the forerunner of Tōyō University, and in 1904 he built the Tetsugaku-dō (Hall of Philosophy), enshrining Shakyamuni, Confucius, Socrates, and Immanuel Kant, in Ekota, on the northwestern outskirts of Tokyo. Enryō strove to revive the tradition of Eastern philosophy while absorbing the lessons of Western thought, and to that end he made three study trips to the West. His influence on the Japanese intelligentsia was considerable, and many of his students became intellectual leaders.

Enryō's best-known writings are *Shinri kinshin* [The Guiding Principle of Truth; 1886–87] and *Bukkyō katsu ron* [Enlivening Buddhism; 1887–90]. In these works he sharply criticized Christianity and emphasized the superiority of Buddhism. He adopted the "scientific" approach popular at the time to refute Christianity.

Many Christian doctrines, he argued, contradict scientific truth, in particular those of a supreme deity and creation. Buddhism made no assertion regarding the existence of God, and its theory of cause and effect agreed with modern scientific concepts. Thus, Enryō concluded, Buddhism's truth was confirmed by science. This manifesto heartened Japanese Buddhists, who had been troubled by Christianity precisely because of its cultural association with scientific Western civilization.

A reaction to Enryō's thesis was to be expected, however, and it came in the form of the rejection of the evaluation of religions, whether Christianity or Buddhism, in "scientific" terms. For the most part, the refusal to reduce religion to science came from Christian quarters, but some thinkers within the Buddhist establishment, such as Murakami Senshō, sounded the same warning. There were other limitations to Enryō's thought. One was his adoption of the slogan "Protect the nation and love the truth." To "love the truth," of course, was an expression of his intellectual passion; but the phrase "protect the nation," though it can be rationalized as referring to the natural bond we feel for the land of our birth, given its historical context suggests sympathy with the pro-imperial, anti-Christian movement of the times. Even if we grant that the contemporary political climate is bound to exert an influence on any thinker, it is regrettable that Enryō could not transcend those limitations.

The greatest assault on Christianity as an "un-Japanese religion" was now launched. It began with the promulgation of the Imperial Rescript on Education on October 30, 1890. A copy of the Imperial Rescript was posted in every school, and the school day began with a bow to it and to the emperor's portrait. When the Imperial Rescript was installed at the First Higher Middle School, in Tokyo, on January 9, 1891, one teacher, Uchimura Kanzō (1861–1930), who became a major force in Japanese Christianity, refused to bow, claiming that as a Christian he owed reverence to God alone. He was widely criticized for his stand, which was considered disrespectful to the emperor. He was finally forced to resign and suffered the rest of his life for his convictions. But similar incidents continued to occur across the nation, and eventually debate arose, led by the philosopher Inoue Tetsujirō (1855–1944).

Inoue Tetsujirō, who headed the Department of Philosophy at Tokyo Imperial University, criticized Christians' refusal to pay reverence to the emperor in a series of articles titled "Kyōiku to shūkyō no shōtotsu" [The Clash of Education and Religion], published in 1894 and 1895 in the journal *Kyōiku jiron* [Views on Education]. He claimed that Christianity, a transcendental religion that taught universal compassion, was incompatible with the "this-worldly" spirit of Japan, which was based on the loyalty of the people to their leaders. In defense of his thesis he frequently quoted Buddhist sources, thus representing Buddhism as typical of the "Japanese spirit" expressed in the Imperial Rescript. Another effect of this tactic was to suggest the superiority of Buddhism to Christianity.

Inoue Tetsujirō claimed that although some transcendental tendencies could be observed in Buddhism, it also taught such doctrines as the Four Objects of Gratitude (*shi on;* there are various enumerations, but most include service to parents, teachers, and the nation's rulers) and thus was not un-Japanese in spirit. He also pointed out that Buddhism asserted the inferiority of women to men and that it recognized a plurality of deities, as did the ancient Japanese myths. Christianity, on the other hand, taught the equality of the sexes and was monotheistic, two principles that could find no home in Japan. He added, however, that Buddhism would have to abandon its world-denying tendency if it wished to become a "civilized religion." In sum, Inoue Tetsujirō merely used Buddhism to support his nationalist arguments, and he rejected Christianity basically on the grounds that it was unpatriotic.

The constitution of the new government, known as the Meiji Constitution, went into effect on February 11, 1889. Article 28 ensured the Japanese people freedom of religious belief "within limits not prejudicial to peace and order, and not antagonistic to their duties as subjects." This article, later invoked to restrict freedom of religion and thought, clearly reveals the limitations of the constitution. Inoue Tetsujirō, in fact, cited this article in his criticism of Christianity.

Of course Japanese Christians objected to Inoue Tetsujirō's criticisms. Many Buddhists, on the other hand, pleased with his praise of their religion, published his writings in their magazines and newspapers and joined his attack on Christianity. Some, however, were bitter about the Buddhist establishment's opportunism. One such critic was the literary figure Takayama Chogyū (1871–1902). At the beginning of his career Takayama was a fervent patriot who rejected both Christianity and Buddhism in favor of Shintō, which he regarded as the Japanese national religion. Later, however, he became a follower of Nichiren's teachings and abandoned his nationalist stance in favor of emphasis on Buddhism as a world religion.

Takayama pointed out the Buddhist establishment's error in joining the attack on Christianity and, interestingly, did so before his change of heart. In *Meiji shisō no hensen* [The Evolution of Meiji Thought; 1898] he argued that as a universal religion Buddhism was in the same position as Christianity with regard to Japan and that both were equally incompatible with Japanese nationalism. He recommended that the two religions cooperate, since "the enemies of Buddhism are the enemies of Christianity." That the Buddhists uncritically "follow Inoue [Tetsujirō] in attacking the Christians" he founded "exceedingly strange."

We can, to some extent, understand the nationalism of the period, which was in part, at least, a response to the perceived need to strengthen the nation, threatened as it was by the encroachment of strong foreign powers. The Buddhists, meanwhile, felt a natural need to rally their forces after the anti-Buddhist movement of the early Meiji years. Nevertheless, in view of Buddhism's essential character as a world religion, they should have heeded Takayama's words. In fact, after the controversy surrounding the publication of Inoue Tetsujirō's "Kyōiku to shūkyō no shōtotsu," some Buddhist leaders did awaken to the true nature of Buddhism as a universal religion and sought to articulate a Buddhist spirit that transcended the narrow confines of Japanese nationalism.

The Christian response was to move toward Japanization, making efforts to send down roots into Japanese society and life. There had been a tendency to view Christianity as an elite phenomenon associated with the West; the Japanization of Christianity was in general a beneficial development for the religion, but at the same time the universal character of Christianity receded as Japanese Christians were caught up in the surge of nationalism that accompanied the Sino-Japanese War (1894–95). The arrival in Japan of new theological concepts and methodology also caused confusion among believers, and the progress of the church became increasingly problematic.

Aside from that, the vigorous debate between Christianity and first Buddhism, then Shintō as well, provided a new forum for dialogue among adherents of these religions. On September 26, 1896, the first interfaith colloquy in Japan was convened, and on December 14 that year, through the efforts of Anesaki Masaharu (1873–1949) and Kishimoto Nobuta (1865–1928), both scholars of religion, the first seminar on comparative religion was held.

The awakening of the Buddhist establishment and the subsequent movement to revitalize the religion were the result of efforts on three fronts: scholarly research, individual thought, and groups of like-minded individuals. As mentioned in chapter 13, one of the main results of the new scholarly study of Buddhism, which included research on early texts and historical study of the canon, was a call for the rejection of Mahayana Buddhism and a return to early, or fundamental, Buddhism. The most talented Japanese Buddhist scholars were pursuing research on those subjects. Anesaki, for example, who pioneered religious studies at Tokyo Imperial University, stated in the preface to his *Genshimbutsu to hosshimbutsu* [Nirmana-kaya and Dharma-kaya; 1901] that the eternal truth was to be found in historical reality; and in *Kompon bukkyō* [Fundamental Buddhism; 1910] he searched for authentic sermons of the Buddha in the Pali scriptures.

Murakami Senshō also rejected the superiority of Mahayana Buddhism and sought to unify the religion in accordance with the tenets of early Buddhism. This caused him trouble with the Jōdo Shin establishment, and his status as a priest was temporarily revoked. But Murakami's position differed somewhat from that of other contemporary Buddhist scholars. He advocated not the abandonment of Mahayana Buddhism but identification of the thread of Buddhist principles that runs through all sects and all texts. This, he held, was the core truth of Buddhism around which all sects could be unified.

That approach obviously led Murakami off the path of strict textual research. But from a wider philosophical viewpoint, it was the only way to clarify the central teachings of Shakyamuni and the religion he founded. Even the earliest Buddhist texts, after all, were composed long after the Buddha's death and may be as far removed from his original teachings as the later Mahayana texts. Thus it is impossible to know conclusively what the Buddha actually taught through textual research alone.

The only way to overcome the limitations of the old texts and sects and revitalize Buddhism was to investigate and compare their teachings and, keeping or discarding traditional elements as appropriate, locate the basic principles to be found in all forms of Buddhism and restructure them in a new intellectual and religious framework. This was done by individuals like Kiyozawa Manshi (1863–1903) and Takayama Chogyū.

Kiyozawa, the son of a warrior, began to study medicine but quit to become a priest of the Ōtani subsect of the Jōdo Shin sect. He was sent to Tokyo Imperial University, where he studied philosophy as an undergraduate and the philosophy of religion in graduate school. In 1888, at the age of twenty-five, he became the principal of the Jōdo Shin sect's Kyoto Middle School. At the same time he taught Western philosophy and the philosophy of religion at Takakura College, affiliated with the Ōtani subsect. After two years in these positions, however, he had a religious awakening and resigned his post at the middle school, shaved his head, discarded Western dress for a priest's robe, and began a life of severe religious discipline. It is believed that a strong desire for enlightenment led him to adopt this way of life.

Kiyozawa's increasingly strenuous austerities led to malnutrition, and he contracted tuberculosis in 1894, at the age of thirty-one. After a two-year recovery and convalescence period, he launched a reform movement and, from his base in Shirakawa, near Kyoto, criticized his sect for its corruption and worldliness. He deplored, for example, the fact that the chief abbot of Hongan-ji had accepted the title of count and kept a concubine. But his reform movement met with little success, and this drove him to still deeper introspection. He began to study the early Buddhist scriptures known as the Agamas and was also attracted to the reflective *Discourses* of Epictetus. He made these two works, together with the *Tanni shō* [Lamenting the Deviations], a collection of Shinran's sayings compiled by a direct disciple, his "three scriptures."

In 1900, at the age of thirty-seven, Kiyozawa began to live communally with like-minded friends in Tokyo. The commune, called the Kōkōdō (Vast Cavern), published a magazine named *Seishinkai* [Spiritual World]. In its pages Kiyozawa advocated what he called "spiritualism" (*seishinshugi*). His last work, *Waga shinnen* [My Beliefs], was published in 1903, the year of his death at the age of forty. His disciples continued the spiritualist movement, but it expired when *Seishinkai* ceased publication in 1918.

Kiyozawa's spiritualism was extremely introspective, and he was criticized by outsiders for giving his "new Buddhism" such a form. We will examine specific points of dissent in the following chapter and here note only that Kiyozawa represented new growth in the tradition of Japanese Buddhist thought. Takayama Chogyū presents an illuminating contrast to Kiyozawa, but since he was a follower of Nichiren's teachings, we will treat his contributions separately.

CHAPTER FIFTEEN

The New Buddhism and
the First Wave of New Religions

Kɪʏᴏᴢᴀᴡᴀ Mᴀɴꜱʜɪ distinguished three phases in the development of Meiji Buddhism: the laicization of Buddhism in the
first decade of the Meiji era, the scholarly and philosophical response to Christianity in the second decade, and the discovery of
the true essence of faith in the third. These divisions are fairly accurate, as we will see as we trace the evolution of Japanese Buddhism during these decades.

As already mentioned, in the early years of the Meiji era many
Buddhist priests traveled to Europe and, under the influence of
Western civilization, initiated a movement to reform Japanese
Buddhism. They sent reports and instructions back from Europe.
For example, since concubinage was considered barbarous in
Europe, they advised that the chief abbot of Hongan-ji dispense
with his concubine. When the Popular Rights Movement, aimed at
democratizing the government along Western lines, began around
1874, many Japanese Buddhists responded to its call and some even
urged the establishment of a republic, a demand that resulted in
their arrest and punishment.

Even Ōuchi Seiran, who later made "Revere the emperor and
serve the Buddha" his slogan, was a progressive thinker at this time.
He founded an organization called the Wakeikai (Society for Harmony and Respect) and lectured actively on the subject of freedom
in religion, education, and politics—even running afoul of official-

dom on occasion and being forced to suspend his activities. But this "advocacy Buddhism" was not based on deep convictions; it was more a fad. When the Popular Rights Movement was broken by the government, Buddhist thinkers abandoned liberal causes and aligned themselves with nationalist and imperialist forces.

Though traces of the influences of the human rights movement can be detected in the 1889 Meiji Constitution, as a whole the document provided a framework for the system of imperial rule; the nationalists, who regarded the emperor as absolute, were in the ascendancy. The Buddhist establishment aligned itself with them and, with nationalism as a weapon, attacked Christianity as un-Japanese while defending itself as part of Japanese tradition.

Inoue Enryō's "scientific" criticism of Christianity suggests at first the modern spirit of enlightened rationalism, but he remained far removed from true democratic liberalism, and thus his writings were easily exploited to attack Christianity in the interest of defending the state. The Buddhist establishment attacked Christianity en masse after Uchimura Kanzō's refusal to bow to the Imperial Rescript and the emperor's portrait and the subsequent publication of Inoue Tetsujirō's "Kyōiku to shūkyō no shōtotsu." Enryō joined the attack with a polemic titled *Chūkō katsu ron* [Reviving Loyalty and Filial Piety; 1893]. Even Murakami Senshō, who had taken issue with Enryō's "scientific" criticism of Christianity, cast his lot with the anti-Christian forces on this occasion, contributing a work titled *Bukkyō chūkō ron* [Loyalty and Filial Piety in Buddhism; 1893].

In the third decade of the Meiji era the first signs of reflection appeared. Buddhist thinkers moved in two directions: toward self-examination and toward social reform. Kiyozawa Manshi and his spiritualism were representative of the former trend, the lay Buddhists who formed the New Buddhist Friends' Association (Shin Bukkyōto Dōshikai) of the latter. It has been suggested that Kiyozawa's sudden conversion to a life of rigorous asceticism was a result of his disenchantment with Enryō's "scientific" and nationalistic criticism of Christianity, but Kiyozawa was also introspective by nature, and his formulation of the principles of spiritualism moved many.

The New Buddhist Friends' Association (originally named the Buddhist Pure Believers' Association [Bukkyō Seito Dōshikai]), was founded in February 1899 by the lay Buddhists Sakaino Kōyō, Takashima Beihō, and Sugimura Sojinkan and the priest Watanabe Kaigyoku. Most members were in their twenties, and many had studied at Inoue Enryō's Tetsugaku-kan. The association's main tenets were strong religious faith, social welfare, intellectual freedom, an end to superstition, abandonment of obsolete Buddhist institutions, and elimination of government interference in religion. Critical of both government policies and the Buddhist establishment, it aimed at the setting up of a progressive society and progressive Buddhism.

Sakaino explained the association's tenets in the magazine *Shin bukkyō* [New Buddhism], which began publication in July 1900. The new Buddhism he advocated was to be oriented toward the concerns of this world, highly principled, enjoyable, free, active, liberal, and dedicated to equality. The old Buddhism was, of course, just the opposite. In particular, while the old Buddhism was a religion of death, the new Buddhism was to be a religion of life. Nor did he see any need for clergy.

The New Buddhist Friends' Association interacted with Christians on an equal footing and encouraged Christians to contribute to *Shin bukkyō*. The group enjoyed an especially close relationship with Japanese Unitarians, who were more liberal than many other Christians. The Unitarians described the New Buddhist Friends' Association and themselves as "the two shoots of new religion in Japan" and called for solidarity to revitalize the Japanese religious world. The New Buddhist Friends' Association, however, preserved the distinction between Buddhism and Christianity in matters of fundamental doctrine. It also criticized Kiyozawa's spiritualism as a philosophy of weakness, in contrast to its own stance of social action—a stance that led to much interaction with the Japanese socialist movement.

The beginnings of the socialist movement and socialist political parties can be traced back to the time of the Sino-Japanese War, when Japanese capitalism made great advances. Backed by nationalist forces, a privileged capitalist class and the great conglomerates known as zaibatsu arose. At the same time, of course, a class of exploited and impoverished workers was created, and tension between these two forces grew. The emergence of monopolistic capitalism, accompanying the establishment of an imperial state, exacerbated conflict between labor and management. National development progressed, but the human cost was great, as the number of low-wage workers grew. Their poverty and frustration finally erupted in strikes, which were ruthlessly put down by the government. Volunteer workers did their best to aid the poor, but the socialists held that the people could not truly be helped unless the very structure of society was reformed.

Eventually the socialists established a political party. The first step in that direction occurred when the Christian socialists Katayama Sen (1860–1933) and Kinoshita Naoe (1869–1937), the Unitarians Abe Iso'o (1865–1949), Kishimoto Nobuta (1865–1928), and Murai Tomoyoshi (1861–1944), the socialist leader Kōtoku Shūsui (1871–1911), and others formed the Society for the Study of Socialism (Shakaishugi Kenkyūkai) in October 1898. The Social Democratic Party (Shakai Minshutō), the first socialist party in Japan, was founded in May 1901. Katayama is also regarded as the father of the Japanese labor movement. In July 1897 he founded the Society for Formation of Labor Unions (Rōdō Kumiai Kiseikai).

Later Kōtoku, influenced by the anarchist movement, began to stress direct political action. He was arrested in 1910 on charges of plotting to assassinate the emperor. The next year he and other alleged conspirators were executed. One surprising fact about this incident is the number of Buddhist priests involved to one degree or another. Uchiyama Gudō, a Sōtō Zen priest, was sentenced to death; Mineo Setsudō, a Rinzai Zen priest, and Takagi Kemmyō, a Jōdo Shin priest of the Ōtani subsect, were sentenced to life imprisonment.

Even before that, the socialist movement had been the object of official persecution on numerous occasions. The Buddhist establishment, while attempting to ease the plight of the people through charitable activities, had either adopted a noncommittal stance toward the imperial state or had followed its dictates. When the priests mentioned above were implicated in the alleged assassination plot, they were expelled from their sects.

Some Buddhists, however, favored the socialists. The members of the New Buddhist Friends' Association were perhaps the prime example of this trend, and in fact some of the participants in the alleged plot were members. But most Buddhist socialists opposed violence on religious grounds and should be regarded as advocates of social reform rather than radical socialists. Moreover, unlike the Christians, some of whom had concrete plans for an ideal society, the Buddhists were vague about what they wished to achieve. Even the members of the New Buddhist Friends' Association were unable to define clear social goals, and the good intentions of the Buddhist socialists were largely theoretical. In 1915 the New Buddhist Friends' Association ceased publication of *Shin bukkyō* and disbanded, partly because of continued pressure by the authorities to obstruct the magazine's sales.

The activities of the so-called new religions provide an interesting contrast to those of the established Buddhist sects of this time. For the purposes of this discussion, "new religion" refers to a religious group centered on the teachings of a charismatic individual. Of course, in most new religions old ideas and beliefs are mingled with new, but the original doctrines of the founder remain crucial identifying features.

We can divide the new religions into two groups: those that arose toward the end of the Edo period and those that came into being in and after the Meiji era. Their doctrinal bases derive from two main lineages: Shintō and Nichiren Buddhism. We will begin by examining Shintō-derived new religions founded in the late Edo period.

Though Fuji *kō*, discussed in chapter 13, was based on traditional mountain worship and could not really claim a historical founder, it was in many ways a precursor of the first wave of new religions. The strength of Fuji *kō*'s roots in the lives of the people was also characteristic of these new religions, the most prominent of which were Kurozumikyō, Tenrikyō, and Konkōkyō.

Kurozumikyō was founded in 1814 by Kurozumi Munetada (1780–1850), a Shintō priest in what is now Okayama Prefecture. When he was thirty-four, he became gravely ill with a lung disease. He worshiped the rising sun and claimed to have achieved union with the solar deity, Amaterasu Ōmikami. He believed that this mystical experience had cured him, and began to preach the benefits of the worship of Amaterasu. He regarded her as the source of all life and human souls as "spiritual particles" thereof. He advocated reliance on "sun energy" to achieve union with her, which would assure health and a better life. An emphasis on "sun energy" is also found in Tenrikyō and Konkōkyō. Munetada also taught that the self must be abandoned, another doctrine common to the other two new religions.

Munetada's first converts were mainly warriors of the local domain, but gradually his teaching spread through southwestern Japan and diffused among the landed, merchant, and artisan classes. After his death his disciple Akagi Tadaharu carried the teachings to Kyoto, where he made many converts among the court nobility and where a shrine to Munetada was built. This shrine, incidentally, became a center for antishogunate forces.

In 1871 the government prohibited the propagation of Kurozumikyō on the grounds that "spells and incantations" were forbidden and in 1874 ordered Kurozumikyō to amend this part of its teaching, but the next year, when the Shintō Office (Shintō Jimukyoku; later the Bureau of Shintō [Shintō Honkyoku]) was established, Kurozumikyō was placed under its jurisdiction. The religion was granted independence in 1876 and classified as a Sectarian Shintō (Kyōha Shintō) religion—the first of thirteen groups to be so recognized.

Tenrikyō was founded in 1838 by Nakayama Miki (1798–1887). She was the wife of Nakayama Zembei, a landlord in what is now Tenri City, Nara Prefecture. Miki had been a devout *nembutsu* believer since childhood. Dire circumstances—the deaths of two daughters, the illness of her oldest son—led her to consult a local shaman (*kitōshi*). As the shaman prayed, Miki was possessed by a spirit claiming to be "the great general of heaven," who had descended to earth to assist "the three thousand realms." Tenri-kyō believers date the founding of their religion to this experience.

After Miki's possession, her family's fortunes declined still fur-ther, but even in her reduced circumstances she continued to spread her message in nearby villages. She wrote *Mikagura-uta* [The Songs for the Service] between 1866 and 1875 and *Ofudesaki* [The Tip of the Divine Writing Brush] between 1869 and 1882. In these works she described the great parent deity Tenri Ō no Mikoto (Lord of Divine Wisdom) and taught that all human be-ings are his children, emphasizing human fellowship and world-wide salvation. She advocated what she called *yōki-gurashi* (joyous life) and maintained that the self is simply a form borrowed from God. She identified eight "dusts," or pollutions, that need to be re-moved from the mind and encouraged hard work and the diligent execution of one's duties.

Though Tenri Ō no Mikoto clearly derives from the *tenrin ō* (*cakravartin*, or "wheel-rolling king") of the Buddhist cosmos, the other doctrines of Tenrikyō derive from Shintō. Despite this mix-ture of traditional beliefs and elements, the strong emphasis in Tenrikyō on salvation for ordinary people and *yo naoshi*, or world renewal, mark it as a new religion. It should also be remembered that it was during Miki's lifetime that the *okage mairi* and *Ee ja nai ka* movements swept Japan.

Tenrikyō was first investigated by the authorities in 1874 and was subjected to repeated persecution thereafter. Miki stood up to the authorities, however, and continued to work in behalf of the people. Feeling that the time for the salvation of humanity was ap-proaching, she began construction of a monument called the *kan-rodai* at the sacred spot (*ojiba*) in her house marking the center of the ideal world to come. She also related a creation myth, the *doroumi kōki* (ancient record of the sea of mud). In 1882 the police carried off the building materials for the *kanrodai*, and the *doroumi kōki* was later banned for contradicting the official Japanese mythology.

Tenrikyō was recognized as a religion in 1885 and placed under the jurisdiction of the Bureau of Shintō. In the winter of the following year, however, Miki was arrested and held for twelve days. This was her eighteenth arrest. Imprisonment took its toll, and she died in February 1887 at the age of eighty-eight. Considerable time passed before Tenrikyō was granted independence from the Bureau of Shintō. In 1908 Tenrikyō was finally recognized as a Sectarian Shintō religion, the last of the new religions to gain that status.

Konkōkyō was founded in 1859 by Kawate Bunjirō (1814–83), a peasant in what is now Okayama Prefecture. A man of deep religious faith, he participated in *okage mairi* and made a pilgrimage to eighty-eight sacred sites on the island of Shikoku. He felt special reverence for the deity Konjin, a fierce god in the pantheon of the Sino-Japanese On'yōdō (Way of Yin and Yang) system. One after another of his children died of illness, and at the age of forty-one he himself fell gravely ill. Fearing that Konjin had cursed him, he prayed for forgiveness. After that Konjin often possessed him, and he received messages from the deity. He came to believe that Konjin was not a vengeful deity but a deity of love. Bunjirō gave Konjin the new name of Tenchi Kane no Kami (Golden Deity of Heaven and Earth). In 1859 he retired from worldly affairs and made his six-mat living room a shrine. He spent the rest of his life there, mediating between people and the deity. Because he performed this divine function, he himself was revered as the *ikigami* (living *kami*) Konkō Daijin (Great Deity of Golden Light).

Tenchi Kane no Kami is the parent of all humankind; from the emperor to the lowliest subject, all are equal before him. Konkō Daijin emphasized the interdependence of God and his believers: "God lives for his children, and they live for God." He taught that the sufferings of the people are the sufferings of God, and that helping people helps God. Mediating between people and God helps both. Konkō Daijin also declared that whomever God grants a divine name becomes a living *kami*. There is no need to fear inauspicious directions or days; all that is necessary is to do God's will as communicated by the medium. There is considerable sophistication in much that Konkō Daijin taught, in particular his thoughts on God, human equality, and mediation between people and God.

Konkōkyō, like the other new religions, suffered under the repressive policies of the Meiji government. It was placed under the jurisdiction of the Bureau of Shintō in 1885 and granted independence as a Sectarian Shintō religion in 1900.

In general, despite their somewhat naive admixture of folk beliefs and their unsophisticated ways of presenting them, these three new religions taught much that was of value. They were closely linked to the common people and devoted to their liberation and the improvement of their lives. Yet these commendable aspects were to be obscured by the growth of nationalism in later years.

Almost all the new religions of Buddhist lineage derived from the Nichiren sect or faith in the Lotus Sutra. This is of considerable interest, but of even greater interest is the fact that we can detect three strands of Nichiren faith. The first was nationalistic, Nichiren being regarded as the pillar of Japanese nationalism. The second transcended nationalism and was universal, seeking to apprehend the true nature of the universe through the teachings of Nichiren and the Lotus Sutra. The third was the organization of new groups of lay believers.

Tanaka Chigaku (1861–1939) exemplified the nationalistic interpretation of Nichiren's teachings. He was born in Edo, the son of a doctor. His father was a fervent follower of Nichiren's teachings, and Tanaka entered a Nichiren-sect temple at the age of nine after his father's death, as his father had wished. At the age of eighteen, however, he became dissatisfied with the priestly life and returned to lay status. At that time he inaugurated his own Nichiren movement. He was convinced that "exalting the national polity" was the basic principle of Nichiren faith.

Tanaka founded the Risshō Ankoku Kai (Society for Establishing the Correct Teaching and Pacifying the Nation) in 1884. In 1889, after the Meiji Constitution was promulgated, he lectured on the new constitution at a series of meetings. In 1894, following the outbreak of the Sino-Japanese War, he established the Kokutō-e (Society to Pray for the Nation), identifying the Eternal Buddha of the Lotus Sutra with Amaterasu Ōmikami and the emperor and praying that the emperor would eliminate the Manchu rulers of China. In 1901 he published *Shūmon no ishin* [The Restoration of Religion], in which he urged the erection of a "great ordination platform of the central teachings of the Lotus Sutra," which he envisaged as a means of establishing the national religion of imperial Japan as the unifying religion of the world and as a place of pilgrimage for worshipers from all nations.

Tanaka's writings were extremely inflammatory. He urged that Japan take Nichiren as its "great general" and the Lotus Sutra as its sword and invade and conquer in order to destroy false beliefs and establish righteousness. When the Russo-Japanese War (1904–5) broke out, he founded another Kokutō-e to pray for victory. He also published *Sekai tōitsu no tengyō* [The Divine Mission to Unify the World] and distributed copies to soldiers heading for the front. In *Nichiren Shōnin no kyōgi* [The Doctrines of Nichiren], published in 1910, he outlined his ideal: the establishment of a "world ordination platform" through the unification of the government and Buddhism. In 1911, following the alleged assassination plot involving Kōtoku Shūsui, he wrote an essay urging the populace to reflect on this treasonous incident and awaken to the need to revere the emperor and protect the nation, and distributed it widely. He also advocated what he called *kokutaigaku*, or the study of the national polity. In 1914 he founded the Kokuchū Kai (Pillar of the Nation Society), through which he continued aggressively to proclaim the need to establish the True Law of Buddhism and exalt the nation.

Had Tanaka been asked which was more important to him, the True Law or national security, no doubt he would have said the former. Yet his leap of logic from Japan's connection with the True Law (the Lotus Sutra) to exaltation of Japan over all other nations led his brand of Nichiren faith to endorse ultranationalism. In fact, many military men and rightists were followers of his. Whatever we may think of his views, however, his influence was widespread.

The second type of Nichiren belief was personified by Takayama Chogyū. While still a student at Tokyo Imperial University,
he wrote a prize-winning historical novel, *Takiguchi nyūdō* [Takigu-
chi the Priest; 1894], and he continued to be active as a writer and
a perceptive literary critic. He was swept up in patriotic fervor
from 1897 to 1900, and during that period criticized both Buddhism and Christianity as otherworldly and un-Japanese. But he
was to undergo a great change.

In August 1900 he suffered a serious lung hemorrhage followed
by deep depression, and began to search for something powerful
to cling to. His convalescence gave him an opportunity for reflection and introspection. During that time he came to feel differently
about religion, which he had rejected until then. His gaze rose
above the nation and its people to a universal realm. He read
Tanaka Chigaku's *Shūmon no ishin* and was struck by the powerful
effect Nichiren seemed to have had in making Tanaka the fire-
brand he was. Takayama turned to Nichiren, as well. In 1901 he
wrote a book about Nichiren's exile to the island of Sado, and
from then on wrote frequently on Nichiren's life and thought.

Takayama was always grateful to Tanaka for introducing him to
Nichiren, but he parted ways with Tanaka on the issue of nationalism. Takayama adopted a stance that transcended nationalism;
it was the universal aspect of Nichiren that appealed to him. In a
work published in 1902, *Nichiren to Kirisuto* [Nichiren and Christ],
he quoted Nichiren's statement "Though, born in the ruler's
realm, I must follow his dictates in my actions, I do not have to follow them in my belief" and the Biblical passage "Render therefore unto Caesar the things which are Caesar's; and unto God the
things that are God's," and declared that if he met anyone who
spoke like this, he would kneel at his feet and beg to become his
disciple. In another work published the same year, *Nichiren Shōnin to
Nipponkoku* [Nichiren and the Japanese Nation], he stated that it
was wrong to regard Nichiren as a nationalist, that to Nichiren the
truth was always far greater than the nation. And in a letter to
Tanaka dated March 27, 1902, Takayama wrote of his doubts
concerning Tanaka's concept of the state.

Takayama's praise of Nichiren influenced many, and societies devoted to Nichiren sprang up across the country. Takayama's former classmate Anesaki Masaharu, who had felt an antipathy toward Nichiren, became a believer under Takayama's influence, lecturing on Nichiren at Tokyo Imperial University and writing the masterpiece *Hokekyō no gyōja Nichiren* [Nichiren, the Man Who Lived the Life of the "Lotus of Truth"].

There was a very clear difference between Tanaka's and Takayama's approaches to Nichiren's fundamental principle of action: transcending the limits of the nation to regulate and reform it. Tanaka's was nationalist, Takayama's supranationalist. This dichotomy illustrates the limits of Japanese Buddhist thinkers at that time. Their critical awareness of the nation and society was still relatively undeveloped in comparison with that of Christians and of socialists sympathetic to Nichiren.

The third offshoot of Nichiren's teachings, new lay groups, began with the Hommon Butsuryū Kō. This was originally associated with the Happon (Hommon) subsect of the Nichiren sect, so strictly speaking it did not constitute a new religion. Still, as a lay movement that sought to escape the abuses of the clergy and the Buddhist establishment, it can be recognized as the source of later Nichiren-related new religions.

The Hommon Butsuryū Kō was typical of the lay assemblies that grew in popularity toward the end of the Edo period. It was founded by Nagamatsu Seifū (also known as Nissen; 1817–90), who was born into a commoner family in Kyoto. Though his family belonged to the Jōdo sect, at the age of twenty-eight he affiliated himself with the Nichiren-sect temple Honnō-ji. Three years later he took the tonsure but soon decided to return to lay status and work for reform of the sect. In 1857 he established a group of lay believers called the Butsuryū Kō, which he developed out of the Happon Kō (eight-chapter assembly) that already existed within the sect.

Seifū devised skillful means for leading lay believers through a variety of levels of faith and understanding. To make the doctrines of the Lotus Sutra easier for lay believers to grasp, he recast them in the form of songs. He also abandoned recitation of the Lotus Sutra in favor of the practice of chanting its title. Meetings were held at different believers' homes in turn. At these gatherings they listened to sermons and discussed their problems and concerns. Considerable emphasis was placed on obtaining worldly benefits through faith. When a member fell ill, for example, he or she chanted the title of the Lotus Sutra, and other members gathered and chanted for the patient. The water placed on the household Buddhist altar was regarded as holy and was given to the patient to drink. Seifū was arrested in 1868 on suspicion of being a Christian. He was persecuted frequently thereafter and spent some time in prison.

Another religious group, an amalgam of Nichiren faith and Shintō called Remmonkyō, arose at the start of the Meiji era. It flourished for a time but was persecuted as a heterodox faith-healing cult and eventually died out.

CHAPTER SIXTEEN

The Second Wave of New Religions

THE DEVELOPMENT OF CAPITALISM in Europe was originally a movement toward democratization and freedom, since it undermined the static class distinctions of feudal Europe and permitted members of the working class to improve their lot through their own efforts. But with the industrial revolution and the subsequent mechanization of labor, large amounts of capital became necessary for efficient production and a class of "supercapitalists" appeared, leading to the development of monopolistic capitalism. A new class system was born, with a wide gap between rich and poor, capitalists and workers.

In the early stages of the development of capitalism, there were opportunities for workers and other poor people to accrue wealth through their own efforts, to become capitalists and manage their own enterprises. But the growth of monopoly capitalism caused the gap between rich and poor to widen dramatically; at the same time, supercapitalists began to build monopolistic conglomerates to control and preserve their wealth. As a result of these developments, the disparity between rich and poor, capital and labor, began to function in the same way as had the rigid class distinctions of feudal society. It became extremely difficult for those born poor to improve their lot. Thus, despite its initial role as the harbinger of a freer, more democratic society, capitalism created new class tensions. Western society has long struggled with this tension be-

tween the bright aspirations of democracy and the conflicts produced by capitalism. Japan in the Meiji era experienced similar
tensions.

Monopoly capitalism eventually created problems not only in
Japan but between Japan and the rest of the world. Western nations had expanded their capitalist systems beyond their borders
by acquiring colonies in Africa and Asia to secure natural resources, markets for their finished goods, and wider arenas for in-
vestment. The economic adventures of Western capitalists were
backed, of course, by their governments, usually with military
might, in an imperialistic advance aimed at the complete economic
and political control of the colonized lands.

The sharp sword of Western imperialism was pointed toward
East Asia in the nineteenth century: first at China, then Korea,
and finally Japan. The Japanese were of course deeply unsettled
by this trend and hastily sought appropriate strategies in both domestic and foreign policy. On the domestic front, one of the first
steps the Meiji government took was the introduction and encouragement of Western-style capitalism to stimulate the development
of Japanese industry. Another step was the unification of the nation under the emperor. The first approach was modern, the second ancient; and the widely varying evaluations of the Meiji era
derive largely from this dichotomy. Perhaps the quickest way to
forge a unified modern nation from feudal Japan was to exalt the
emperor. But it led to government by conservative advisers, leaders of clan-based cliques and career bureaucrats, who suppressed
the Popular Rights Movement and blocked the development of
party politics.

In foreign policy, Japan was faced with a choice: either it could
ally itself with China and Korea to resist the pressures from the
West or it could compete with the West in carving out its own
share of East Asian colonies. Japan chose the latter course, thus
becoming part of the imperialistic advance and embroiling itself in
wars of conquest. In the Meiji and Taishō (1912–26) eras alone,
Japan invaded Taiwan (1874), waged war against China (1894–
95), took over Taiwan (1895), went to war with Russia over south-

ern Sakhalin (1904–5), annexed southern Sakhalin (1905), annexed Korea (1910), took part in World War I (1914–18), and sent an expeditionary force to Siberia (1918).

The Western nations sided with or against Japan in these conflicts according to their own interests. In Asia, meanwhile, Indian and Chinese leaders hailed the Japanese victory in the Russo-Japanese War as restoring pride in Eastern civilization. The Japanese colonization of Korea that followed, however, was a great disappointment to the rest of Asia. Japan's aggression marked it as just another imperialistic conqueror grabbing a piece of the Asian pie. Later, when the struggle for international hegemony escalated, Japan would find itself drawn in by its own imperialistic adventures. Japanese participation in World War I is a classic example.

China and Korea were the greatest victims of Japanese imperialism. Even if historical circumstances led Japan to refuse the role of liberator of Asia and become instead one of its worst exploiters, we must recognize this as one of the great stains on the pages of Meiji history. Moreover, instead of wiping this stain away Japan's leaders encouraged it to spread in the following Taishō and Shōwa (1926–89) eras.

Some Japanese leaders during the Meiji era were outspoken imperialists. The prime minister during the Russo-Japanese War and twice afterward, Katsura Tarō, for example, declared, "Domestically we must promote loyalty to the imperial house; on the foreign front we will pursue imperialist policies." The imperialist cause was not, however, without critics. Some members of the Popular Rights Movement emphasized that the road of independence from the West was to be found in alliance with rather than invasion of China and Korea.

The goal of the Popular Rights Movement was to replace government by clan-based cliques and the entrenched bureaucracy loyal to the emperor with a constitutional, parliamentary system and party politics based on elections. These goals seemed to have been attained with the promulgation of the constitution in 1889 and parliamentary elections the next year. Before that, two political parties had been formed, the Liberal Party (Jiyūtō) in 1881 and the Constitutional Reform Party (Rikken Kaishintō) in 1882. But the government persecuted both, and the movement to establish party politics met with great difficulties. The parties were frequently ignored by the bureaucracy. Furthermore, only males at least twenty-five years of age who paid at least ¥15 (a considerable sum at the time) in national taxes could vote, so elections did not reflect the popular will.

With the spread of education, however, an intelligentsia grew up that opposed Japanese imperialism and supported democracy and freedom. In addition, the welfare movement that had arisen to help the poor, the victims of monopoly capitalism, gradually evolved into a full-fledged socialist movement that provided great stimulus to the democratic movement.

Literary movements are a good indicator of contemporary intellectual trends. At first, the development of a modern capitalistic society liberated the Japanese, releasing them from the bonds of feudalism and awakening them to their existence as autonomous individuals. The movement known as Romanticism swept the Japanese literary scene around the time of the Sino-Japanese War. Romanticism soon reached a dead end, however, mainly because it pursued individual freedom through escape from society. The movement was characterized by the idealization of romantic love, emotional rapture, and preoccupation with private pursuits. It lacked the strength to resist oppression and, on the contrary, yielded easily to it.

Naturalism arose in its place around the time of the Russo-Japanese War. Naturalism advocated the annihilation of traditional customs and feudalistic policies and a return to "naked humanity." Naturalism, however, failed to produce any new social forms or structures to take the place of the old. It turned a sharply critical eye on humanity, but when Naturalists collided with the thick wall of reality, they lacked any positive response and tended to sink into despair.

These literary movements reveal the weakness and inexperience of Japan's intelligentsia at the time. Most intellectuals were from the middle class. They lacked the ruthless vigor of the monopoly capitalists and the ruling class on the one hand and the energy of the oppressed working class on the other. This applies to intellectuals today, as well; indeed, it seems to be their constant fate. Nevertheless, it is wrong to conclude that therefore intellectuals were (or are) useless. Their critical spirit helps to steer both society and individuals away from violence and onto constructive paths. Intellectuals play a necessary and even a leading role in history. At the time of the Russo-Japanese War, for example, some intellectuals spoke out against the war and against war in general, and intellectuals later played a formative role in the movement known as Taishō Democracy.

The Taishō era was an exciting and dynamic time, characterized by a rapid succession of events involving all elements of the political spectrum. In 1913 there was a political crisis that forced the resignation of the entire cabinet, made up of bureaucrats with no popular mandate. World War I brought prosperity, but inflation led to a financial panic and widespread rice riots in 1918. In the same year it was decided that all cabinet members had to be members of political parties. In 1920 May Day was first celebrated in Japan, influenced by the Russian Revolution three years earlier, and in 1922 the Japan Communist Party was formed. The Great Kantō Earthquake, which devastated Tokyo, occurred in 1923.

The movement for universal male suffrage resulted in the 1925 amendment of the Election Law to permit all males twenty-five and older to vote, though the repressive Peace Preservation Law, aimed at stifling left-wing dissent, was also passed the same year. Despite this oscillation between left and right, liberal and conservative, the overall trend was toward greater democracy, hence the term Taishō Democracy. In politics, in philosophy, in critical writing, and in literature there was a rising tide of freedom and democracy that produced many significant results. In philosophy, human nature and human life were explored to new depths. In literature, ethics and idealism led the day, exemplified by the Shirakaba (White Birch) school of writers. When these developments combined with broad social trends, they became movements stressing the liberation and equality of all people. In this period, too, feminism was born in Japan.

The nature of the questions intellectuals were asking themselves—What is humanity? What is life? How should it be lived?—led them toward religion, for these are its fundamental concerns. Philosophers and writers incorporated Buddhist and Christian concepts in their works; some even became, in effect, religious leaders. Orthodox religious leaders were influenced by this trend and increased their own efforts, writing and evangelizing, devoting their energies to study and propagation.

The influence of the idealistic Neo-Kantians led to the translation of many Western philosophical works, which stimulated Japanese thinkers to write original works emphasizing humanism, civilization, and liberal education. The commitment to education gave rise to the so-called Education school, as influential in philosophy as the Shirakaba school was in literature. These trends were adopted by intellectuals in general, and the works of a great variety of philosophers were widely read. *Santarō no nikki* [Santarō's Diary; 1914–15] by the Neo-Kantian philosopher Abe Jirō (1883–1959), portraying a young man's search for the meaning of life, is a classic example of philosophical writings of the period that influenced a wide audience—in the case of this work, young people in particular.

As already mentioned, the intellectuals of the Taishō era actively reached out to religion, which they incorporated in their writings, though their emphasis was not faith but a broad-based humanism; religion was studied as part of life and human nature. These activities contributed to a new, more sophisticated understanding of religion that attracted intellectuals. This humanistic interest in religion, however, led to a decline in the vigor of religious faith, since the intellectuals were concerned with theory and aesthetics rather than practice.

The intellectual world was a great salon, with little power to re-

sist the sometimes violent waves of change that were sweeping society. It had distanced itself from the problems of the people, and
here the limits of Taishō Democracy as well as the darker side of
Taishō society are revealed. With the financial panic of 1918, the
contradictions that had been building up beneath the surface of
society erupted. Japan's economic and political systems were
threatened both at home and abroad. Within Japan, popular dissatisfaction took the form of labor unrest; in colonized Korea an
independence movement arose. The government responded with
reactionary resistance and sometimes with violent oppression. For
example, though universal male suffrage was introduced in 1925,
so was the Peace Preservation Law. The intellectuals in the van-
guard of Taishō Democracy as well as ordinary citizens caught in
the middle felt powerless in the face of social unrest and instability
and the forceful measures of the government. A popular song of
1921 expressed this sentiment eloquently: "I am just withered grass
at the river's edge, and you are the same. Neither of us will bloom
in this world."

Several new religions arose around this time in response to the
people's suffering. We will examine two of these, Shintō-based
Ōmoto and Buddhist Reiyūkai, from which other new religions
were to emerge. But first let us look at the activities of the established Buddhist sects at the time.

In May 1904, a few months after the outbreak of the Russo-
Japanese War, Japanese representatives of Shintō, Confucianism,
Buddhism, and Christianity met in Tokyo and issued a declaration
stating that war against Russia was necessary for national security,
peace in Asia, civilization, righteousness, and ethics. Thus the religious establishment, including Buddhists, sanctioned the war.
(Incidentally, in February 1912 the government engineered a "tri-
partite conference" of Shintō, Buddhist, and Christian representatives, finally according Christianity equal status with the other two
religions. The price Japanese Christians paid was support of national policy and the imperial system.) There was no antiwar
protest in the Buddhist camp except for the voices of a rare few,

such as the members of the New Buddhist Friends' Association, Uchiyama Gudō and others implicated in the alleged assassination plot of 1910, and Itō Shōshin (1876–1963), the founder of the *muga ai* (selfless love) movement.

Itō was a priest in the Ōtani subsect of the Jōdo Shin sect, but, becoming convinced that life should be devoted to "selfless love," he left the clergy and initiated a movement to spread his message. During the Russo-Japanese War he opposed war on any grounds, and after Japan's victory he castigated the euphoric public for its blind attachment to self-interest. In 1905 he founded the commune Muga-en (Garden of Selflessness) and began to publish the magazine *Muga no ai* [Selfless Love]. His teaching of freedom from attachment to self through selfless love attracted many followers. The celebrated Marxist economist Kawakami Hajime (1879–1946) was associated with Muga-en for a time. In his concern with human equality and world peace, Itō had much in common with the socialists, with whom he associated. He was imprisoned for writing a defense of Kōtoku Shūsui after his alleged attempt to assassinate the emperor.

Although some outside the Buddhist fold criticized the mainstream Buddhists for failing to protest the Russo-Japanese War, most Buddhists cooperated with the war effort, offering prayers for victory and sending priests to minister to the troops. Buddhists also cared for the wounded and offered assistance to families who had lost men in the war. Though such relief activities were admirable, the lack of objections to the larger issue of war itself reveals the narrow outlook of the Buddhist establishment at that time.

In short, aside from a small number of progressive and socialist Buddhists, such as Itō Shōshin, the Buddhist establishment came down firmly on the side of Japanese imperialism, limiting its religious role to welfare activities. Since these activities filled gaps created by harsh government policies, there was some danger that Buddhism would again become an instrument of official policy. Yet there can be no denying that such assistance was important and welcome to the recipients. The activities of Japanese Buddhists in that area were indeed remarkable. Much attention was also paid to institutional reform, and missionaries began to spread Japanese Buddhism abroad.

As already mentioned, with the flowering of Taishō Democracy Buddhist concepts were incorporated in literature and philosophy, and in that regard Buddhism contributed a great deal to the new age. The philosopher Nishida Kitarō (1870–1945), influenced by the Zen philosopher and exponent Suzuki Daisetsu (known in the West as Daisetz T. Suzuki; 1870–1966) and by Kiyozawa Manshi's spiritualism, created a unique philosophy combining Buddhist concepts with principles of Western philosophy. He gained instant fame with his first work, *Zen no kenkyū* [A Study of Good; 1911]. The playwright and essayist Kurata Hyakuzō (1891–1943) wrote a play about Shinran titled *Shukke to sono deshi* [The Priest and His Disciples; 1916] that was widely read by young people. Influenced by Nishida Kitarō, he also wrote *Ai to ninshiki to no shuppatsu* [The Beginning of Love and Understanding; 1922], which became a classic among the youth of the Taishō era.

The spirit of Taishō Democracy touched Buddhism, as well. New Buddhist journals were published, and Buddhist studies were further stimulated. Efforts were devoted to modernizing the teachings of the various sects and to improving and modernizing their universities. Institutional reform was carried out, and more emphasis was placed on welfare activities. But for the most part the Buddhist establishment had its hands full simply trying to preserve itself and keep up with the times. Serving as a leading force, addressing and resolving the contradictions of contemporary society—these tasks were beyond its resources.

Two non-Buddhist religious developments of the time deserve mention: the commune Ittō-en (Garden of the Single Torch) of Nishida Tenkō (1872–1968) and the Christian social-reform movement of Kagawa Toyohiko (1888–1960). Nishida Tenkō was the son of a paper wholesaler in Shiga Prefecture. He established Ittō-en, a commune whose members espoused the principle of no private property or possessions, in an area of Kyoto called Shishigatani in

1905. He is said to have developed his philosophy of communal living after reading Leo Tolstoy's *Confession*. He used Buddhist terminology to explain his philosophy and regarded "light" (*ohikari*) as the focus of worship and the core of all faiths. The members of Ittō-en dedicated themselves to lives of mendicancy, service, and confession. Their ideal was a world of equality, free of competition for survival, which was to be realized not through social revolution but personal transformation.

In 1921 Nishida Tenkō published *Zange no seikatsu* [The Life of Confession], which captured the imagination of many and made his name and that of his commune known throughout Japan. Ittō-en formed a theater troupe, the Suwaraji Gekidan, and in the mid-1920s members began to travel to China, Korea, the Hawaiian Islands, and North America to spread Nishida Tenkō's teachings. After the commune moved to the Yamashina district of Kyoto in 1928, membership grew to several hundred. Kurata Hyakuzō lived there for a time.

Unlike Nishida Tenkō, who had strong but apolitical convictions, Kagawa Toyohiko devoted his energies to social reform. Kagawa was born into a Kōbe family that owned a steamship line. As a youth he contracted tuberculosis and, while battling the disease, was drawn to Christianity, receiving baptism in 1904. In 1909 he began to live in the Kōbe slums, where he began his proselytization. His autobiographical novel *Shisen o koete* [Crossing the Deathline], published in 1920, became a bestseller. The following year he led the struggle of Kōbe and Kawasaki shipyard workers for better working conditions. He organized a strike of more than thirty-eight thousand workers, which was brutally put down by the military and the police. After the Great Kantō Earthquake of 1923 he established a settlement in Tokyo from which he directed a wide variety of welfare activities. He also traveled to the West to lecture and gained an international reputation. His public antiwar statements led to his arrest by the infamous Kempeitai, or military police, in 1940.

Kagawa, like Nishida Tenkō and many other Taishō religious thinkers, was influenced by Tolstoy in his youth. The Shirakaba literary school, centered on the novelist Mushanokōji Saneatsu (1885–1976), also made Tolstoy's humanism its creed, and Mushanokōji based his utopian commune Atarashiki Mura (New Village) in Miyazaki Prefecture, Kyūshū, on its principles. But the Shirakaba school drew its main support from the middle class, while Kagawa dedicated himself to people of the working class, living among them and working actively for social reform.

Let us now examine the second wave of new religions, focusing on Ōmoto and Reiyūkai. Ōmoto was founded in 1892, when a woman named Deguchi Nao (1836–1918) believed herself to be possessed by a god she called Ushitora no Konjin. She was the daughter of a carpenter in Fukuchiyama, in what is now Kyoto Prefecture. At seventeen she was adopted by her aunt's family, the Deguchis, in Ayabe, also in present Kyoto Prefecture, and two years later she married. Her life in the following decades was hard. In addition to the normal difficulties of raising a family, two of her daughters developed mental problems.

At the age of fifty-six she believed herself to have been possessed by Ushitora no Konjin, "the god who rejuvenates and restores the universe." The year after her possession there was a case of arson in Ayabe, and she was imprisoned as a suspect. In her cell she began to write with a nail on a wooden pillar. This was the beginning of her *ofudesaki* (writings), which eventually amounted to two hundred thousand pages of manuscript. These writings concern the origin and manifestation of the god of Ōmoto (the Great Origin), the creation of the universe, prophecies for humankind, and the duties of the Japanese people. The general emphasis is on *yo naoshi*, world renewal.

After her release from prison Deguchi Nao joined Konkōkyō but left in 1897 to establish her own religion. Since it was not an officially recognized organization, she was harassed by the police, but she continued to proselytize. In 1898 a man named Ueda Kisaburō (later Deguchi Onisaburō; 1871–1948) joined her in her efforts to spread the new religion. He was born into a poor peasant family in Kameoka, Kyoto Prefecture. He became a substitute teacher at the local elementary school as a teenager but quit after two years and supported himself with a series of humble jobs—peddler, servant, milkman, and so forth. When he was twenty-seven he had a vision of a divine spirit and withdrew to the mountains, where he fasted. He claimed that because of his austerities he had been possessed by a spirit whose powers he could transfer to other people. He later wrote of his experiences in *Reikai monogatari* [Tales of the Spirit World].

In 1898, as mentioned, he met Deguchi Nao, and the next year he began to work with her to spread her teachings. She was sixty-three at the time and he twenty-seven. In January 1900 he married Deguchi Nao's youngest daughter, Sumi, and took the Deguchi family name. Three years later he changed his personal name to Onisaburō.

At first Nao and Onisaburō called their organization the Kimmei Reigaku Kai (Golden Brilliance Spiritual Study Group); in 1908 the name was changed to the Dai Nippon Shūsai Kai (Great Japan Purification Society), and in 1916 to Kōdō Ōmoto (Great Fundamentals of the Imperial Way). The new religion gained many followers through the phenomenal success of Onisaburō's proselytization.

Kotani Kimi (1901–71) was one of the founders of Reiyūkai. The daughter of poor peasants in Miura, Kanagawa Prefecture, she married at seventeen, but her husband died soon after and she went to Tokyo to look for work. At the age of twenty-four she married a believer in the Lotus Sutra named Kotani Yasukichi (1895–1929), who as it happens was born in Kominato, Chiba Prefecture, the birthplace of Nichiren. Yasukichi's younger brother, Kakutarō (1892–1944), was adopted by the Kubo family and became an architect for the Imperial Household Ministry. He too was a devout believer in the Lotus Sutra.

In 1923 Kakutarō founded the first Reiyūkai with a woman Lotus Sutra believer, Wakatsuki Chise, at Hokekyō-ji, in the Nakayama district of Ichikawa, Chiba Prefecture. Two years later he reorganized the group together with Yasukichi and Kimi, and they began to proselytize. Kimi devoted herself to practice and exhibited psychic powers that attracted new followers. After Yasukichi's death in 1929 Reiyūkai continued to grow and flourish under the leadership of the other two founders.

Many groups branched off from Ōmoto and Reiyūkai. From Ōmoto grew Sekai Kyūsei Kyō, Seichō no Ie, and Ananaikyō; from Reiyūkai evolved Kōdō Kyōdan, Risshō Kōsei-kai, Myōchi-kai, Bussho Gonen-kai, Myōdō-kai, and Hosshi-kai. In the next chapter we will examine why Ōmoto and Reiyūkai served as a breeding ground for so many other new religions and will trace the development of some of them.

CHAPTER SEVENTEEN

The New Religions and Mainstream Buddhism Before and During World War II

U NDER DEGUCHI ONISABURŌ'S leadership nationalism, inter-nationalism, and identification with the masses became the three pillars of Ōmoto. These principles often clashed, leading to contradictory actions on the part of both Onisaburō and Ōmoto as a whole. At the same time, the coexistence of these sometimes contradictory elements within Onisaburō reveals a man so large in scale that he could embrace extremes.

The year of his marriage to Sumi, 1900, saw the outbreak of the Boxer Rebellion in China, which Japan helped to put down. Tension was rising both within Japan and overseas. While welcoming Japan's display of national prestige, Onisaburō had misgivings about the nation's situation in the light of Ōmoto's underlying philosophy of *yo naoshi* and warned of future dangers, as he did again at the time of the Russo-Japanese War. The *yo naoshi* concept, of course, had developed from the wish of the common people for peace and happiness. Though he prayed for victory, he also opposed war, which claimed so many victims among the people. Onisaburō wrote in his diary that *yo naoshi* was necessary "so that there will be no need for soldiers and no more wars, so that peace will prevail on earth." He also firmly believed that as children of God equal in his sight all men and women were brothers and sisters. Here is revealed one of the contradictions in his thinking: while supporting the Russo-Japanese War and frequently taking a

nationalistic view of the world, he argued against war and declared that all people were equal.

Since Ōmoto was not recognized by the government, it was frequently subjected to police interference. The organization tried to
protect itself by affiliating with a registered Sectarian Shintō organization and changing its name to Dai Nippon Shūsai Kai,
which had a patriotic ring. Its prayers for Japan during the Russo-
Japanese War were another manifestation of these efforts. To attract
followers, Ōmoto offered them satisfaction of their immediate
needs and solutions to their problems, teaching spiritual methods
for curing illness, for example. This last, however, brought Ōmoto
under official suspicion as a "superstitious and heterodox cult"; it
was also a deviation from the *yo naoshi* ideal on which Nao had
based the religion. To boost membership, Onisaburō gradually
tied the fortunes of Ōmoto to national development and overseas
expansion. In this sense, his ideal of reform came to resemble the
right-wing ideal of the "reconstruction of Japan" in the early years
of the Shōwa era (1926–89).

When World War I broke out, Ōmoto warned that the reconstruction of the world was at hand and redoubled its efforts to re-
cruit members. It organized quasi-military preaching units called
chokureigun (literally, "direct spirit troops"). In 1916 the religion
changed its name to Kōdō Ōmoto, "Great Fundamentals of the
Imperial Way," and dispatched *chokureigun* units throughout the
nation. Their members presented a strange sight, with their long
hair, white sashes, and short swords tucked in their belts. They
traveled on horseback, carrying banners and beating drums as
they prophesied a great war between Japan and the rest of the
world and called for "reconstruction."

Onisaburō came to believe that he was the incarnation of
Miroku (Maitreya). In 1920 he purchased a newspaper, the *Taishō
nichinichi shimbun*, and used it to spread the group's doctrines. His
vigorous proselytization, prophetic pronouncements, and heated
call for national reconstruction attracted many to Ōmoto, military
men and students in particular. A number of intellectuals were
also deeply moved by his message and his conviction.

Ōmoto continued to expand, but eventually its prophetic warnings and its prodigious activities led the government to view it with suspicion and alarm. In February 1921 Onisaburō was charged with lèse-majesté and violation of the Newspaper Law. Ōmoto's main worship hall and Nao's tomb were demolished. Onisaburō was imprisoned but was released on bail in June. By 1923 he was busy preparing materials for overseas missions in Esperanto and romanized Japanese, while also forging a cooperative agreement with the Red Swastika Society of China. In 1924, while still officially free on bail, he made a secret trip with several Ōmoto members to Mongolia. The next year Ōmoto spearheaded the creation in Peking of the World Federation of Religions, which included various Chinese religions. Seeking to cooperate with other religions in Japan, as well, Ōmoto founded the Jinrui Aizen-kai (Benevolence for Humankind Association). The purpose of both organizations was to unify the efforts of all religions to create a world in which all people could live in harmony and prosperity.

The first persecution of Ōmoto ended in 1927, when the government decreed a general amnesty, as a result of which the case against Onisaburō was dismissed. In 1928 he announced that the time had come for the advent of Miroku. He presided over a great "Miroku festival," then traveled throughout Japan and, the following year, to Korea and Manchuria to proselytize. Ōmoto missions even spread to Southeast Asia and the Pacific islands, following in the footsteps of Japan's overseas expansion.

A series of reformist right-wing coup attempts occurred in the 1930s. In response to this new mood, Onisaburō founded the Shōwa Shinsei-kai (Shōwa Sacred Society) in July 1934. With the praise and support of patriots, it began to play an active political role. But the government soon felt threatened by this activity, too, and Ōmoto underwent its second major persecution. In 1935 the government investigated more than a thousand members, and arrests and indictments extended to the level of branch head. The headquarters building was dynamited.

Some Ōmoto members died of illness during the long and severe detention pending trial, but Onisaburō was released on bail in 1942, after six years and eight months. Japan was embroiled in World War II, but he took a defiant stance and refused to cooperate with the war effort. He prayed instead for Japan's defeat. He became the focus of widespread public criticism for giving amulets to soldiers heading for the front that contained slips of paper with the message "Victory to the enemy." In 1946, the year following Japan's defeat, he revived Ōmoto under the name Aizen-en (Garden of Love and Virtue). He died in 1948. Since his death the religion, having restored the name Ōmoto in 1952, has continued to work for such causes as world peace and unity, opposition to Japanese rearmament, and the prohibition of nuclear weapons.

Leadership of Ōmoto is hereditary and matrilineal. Onisaburō's wife, Sumi, became the second-generation president after Nao's death, and her daughter Naohi succeeded her. Onisaburō held the lesser title of chairman, but in fact it was he who controlled the organization. In that sense, Ōmoto's activities were greatly influenced by his character, but regarded from a broader perspective, Ōmoto was typical of the new religions that arose in the early decades of the twentieth century. It was also the womb from which several other new religions were born.

One of these was Sekai Kyūsei Kyō (Church of World Messianity), founded by Okada Mokichi (1882–1955). Okada was the son of an antique dealer in Tokyo. A sickly child, he was forced by ill health to leave school without graduating and spent most of his youth battling illness. In his early twenties he opened a sundries shop, but poor health continued to plague him. He became interested in folk medicine and began to devise his own treatments. He made considerable money from stocks during the World War I boom but lost it in the financial panic after the war. His wife died, as well, leaving him in despair. Not long thereafter he happened to attend a lecture on Ōmoto and was deeply moved. He joined Ōmoto and became a missionary in 1928.

After joining Ōmoto, Okada received a series of divine revelations and came to believe that he could cure illness through the power of the bodhisattva Kannon (Avalokiteshvara). He left Ōmoto and in 1935 established the Dai Nihon Kannon Kai (Japan Kannon Society), teaching that illness could be cured by the purifi-catory spiritual power (*jōrei*) emanating from the palm of another person's hand. Okada believed that this healing power was inher-ent in everyone and that its strength depended on one's spiritual progress. Medicines, he declared, were poisons. As a result of his unorthodox healing activities he was charged with violating the Medical Practitioners Law and was arrested and subjected to ha-rassment. Okada also advocated organic farming methods. Actu-ally, views like his were widespread for a time after World War II, in part because of the shortage of medicines and chemical fertilizers.

Okada changed the group's name to Nihon Kannon Kyōdan (Japan Kannon Church) in 1947 and to Sekai Meshiya Kyō (Church of World Messianity) in 1950. (The present name, Sekai Kyūsei Kyō, was adopted in 1957.) Okada taught that Kannon was the savior of the world and would create a paradise on earth free of illness, poverty, and strife. He was regarded as Kannon's representative. The organization constructed models of the par-adise to come in the seaside resort of Atami and in Hakone, near Mount Fuji, and also built art museums there.

Seichō no Ie (House of Growth), founded by Taniguchi Masa-haru (1893–1985), is another offshoot of Ōmoto. Taniguchi was born into a farming family in Kōbe. He began studying English literature at Waseda University but for personal reasons aban-doned his studies without taking a degree. Later, because of illness and poverty, he turned to psychic powers for relief and began studying psychic phenomena. Learning of Ōmoto, he joined the group in 1917. Ōmoto recognized his literary talent, and he be-came an editor of one of its magazines. He sought to emulate Saint Francis of Assisi, living a life of poverty and self-denial. Nevertheless, he used the first great persecution of Ōmoto, in 1921, as an opportunity to break away from the group. In 1929 he claimed to have received a divine revelation, and in 1930 he be-gan publishing the magazine *Seichō no ie* to spread his teachings through the print medium.

Taniguchi taught that there is a life force that is the source of all phenomena, that all religions are essentially the same, and that all people are God's children. He also taught that illness can be healed by spiritual means. Though he stood right of center politically, he attracted many followers with his message of God's love and the realization of a paradise on earth through the power of love.

The postwar group Ananaikyō is also closely related to Ōmoto. It was founded in 1949 by Nakano Yonosuke (1887–1974), who advocated the integration of the teachings of Baha'i, Ōmoto, and the Red Swastika Society with those of Buddhism, Christianity, Confucianism, Islam, and Taoism. (*Ananai* is an ancient Japanese word written with the ideograms for "three" and "five.") Ananaikyō teaches that all people are equal and all religions basically the same, and that religion should serve to unite the world. The group has organized several international conferences on religion.

PL [Perfect Liberty] Kyōdan is a new religion not directly related to Ōmoto. It was founded by Miki Tokuharu (1871–1938), the son of a poor merchant. After his father went bankrupt, Miki entered a temple as a novice at the age of eight, but he left the priesthood in 1915, when he was forty-four. The next year he became a disciple of Kanada Tokumitsu (1863–1919), the founder of Tokumitsukyō, and on Kanada's death succeeded him as head of the organization. In 1925 Miki founded Ontakekyō Tokumitsu Daikyōkai Hombu, changing its name to Fusōkyō Hito no Michi Kyōdan in 1931. Miki gained many followers through his claim to be able to transfer people's afflictions to himself, a practice he had adopted from Tokumitsukyō. In the late 1930s he was convicted of lèse-majesté for teaching that Amaterasu Ōmikami is the sun rather than the solar deity. After World War II Miki Tokuharu's son Tokuchika (1900–1983) revived the group, this time with the name PL Kyōdan. Its central motto is "Life is art."

On the Buddhist end of the spectrum, Reiyūkai attracted many followers with its promise of benefits in this life and its practice of ancestor veneration. Reiyūkai also devised the practice of *hōza* (Dharma circle), a form of religion-centered group counseling that attracted many new members. The first group to split off from

Reiyūkai was Kōdō [Way of Filial Piety] Kyōdan, led by Okano Shōdō and his wife. Okano joined Reiyūkai in 1934 but left the next year to found Kōdō-kai. In 1948 the organization's name was changed to Kōdō Kyōdan. Members of Kōdō Kyōdan revere the Lotus Sutra and chant its title, but the group is now affiliated with the Tendai sect.

Risshō Kōsei-kai was founded by Niwano Nikkyō (1906–) and Naganuma Myōkō (1889–1957). Naganuma was the sixth daughter of an old family in Saitama Prefecture. The family fortunes had declined, however, and she grew up in poverty. Her mother died when she was six, and she went to live with her uncle. At the age of sixteen she was adopted by an older sister, on whose urging she joined Tenrikyō, but she soon left her sister's household and went to Tokyo. There she supported herself by working as a maid and then in an army munitions dump and arsenal but collapsed from overwork and returned to her uncle's house.

She married when she was twenty-six, but her husband led a dissolute life and eventually she divorced him and moved to Tokyo again, where she remarried. Her new husband was an ice wholesaler, and she opened her own shop, dealing in ice in the summer and selling roasted sweet potatoes in the winter. The couple did well, and at last she enjoyed financial stability. But she had been weakened by her many hardships and fell ill. At this juncture, in 1936, a Reiyūkai member who ran a milk shop visited her and urged her to join the group. He was Niwano Nikkyō.

Niwano was the second son of a farming family in Niigata Prefecture. After finishing elementary school he helped out on the farm and continued his education at night school. When he was sixteen he went to Tokyo to work for a rice dealer. After the Great Kantō Earthquake in 1923 he returned to Niigata, but the next year he went to Tokyo again and worked for a charcoal dealer named Ishihara Yoshitarō. Ishihara was adept at divination based on the Chinese classic the *I Ching*, and his enthusiasm spread to Niwano, who took up the study of divination. After serving in the navy, Niwano married. He opened a pickle shop, and in his spare time he studied Shugendō with a woman practitioner in the neighborhood. He also studied divination based on personal names (*seimeigaku*).

The illness of Niwano's second daughter in the summer of 1935 motivated him to join Reiyūkai. Arai Sukenobu, who introduced him to the group, was a devout believer in the Lotus Sutra, and Niwano was deeply influenced by his teaching. After joining Reiyūkai, Niwano decided to open a milk shop because of the opportunities it would give him to proselytize. That was how he met Naganuma and brought her into Reiyūkai.

In 1938 Niwano and Naganuma left Reiyūkai and founded Dai Nippon Risshō Kōsei-kai. In 1948 the name of the organization was shortened to Risshō Kōsei-kai, and in 1960 the character for *kō* (exchange) was changed to the *kō* of Myōkō, in a posthumous tribute to her role as cofounder. Risshō Kōsei-kai has become one of the largest of the Buddhist new religions through the superior leadership of its founders, its vigorous grassroots activities centered on *hōza*, and the freshness and timeliness of its message.

After World War II many other religious organizations branched off from Reiyūkai, and in the next chapter we will consider them, as well as another major Nichiren-based new religion, Sōka Gakkai. Why are all these new religions of Buddhist lineage derived from Nichiren and the Lotus Sutra? The boom times of World War I were short-lived. As the economic picture darkened with the financial panic that followed the war, many workers and tenant farmers found themselves unemployed or forced to work for a pittance. These conditions led to widespread demonstrations and strikes. The socialists and communists sympathized with the plight of the workers and tenant farmers and supported their cause, and the government tried to suppress this surge of leftist activity forcibly.

Meanwhile, some monopoly capitalists pursued plans to protect their own profits with the backing of the government. The eventual result was Japan's military advance into continental Asia, a policy designed to break through the economic and political impasse at home and divert the people's attention to events overseas. The end of World War I had left Britain and the United States dominant in the Orient. The government perceived this as a threat, and the struggles of the Chinese and Koreans against Japanese hegemony also provided a fine excuse for whipping up patriotic fervor. Step by step the government mobilized the nation: the Manchurian Incident (1931), the Marco Polo Bridge Incident (1937), and finally World War II.

Young right-wing army officers tried several times to overthrow the government in the 1930s. Their attempts finally resulted in the triumph of the militarists, but the young officers who led the coup attempts had other motives. They were alarmed by the desperate plight of farmers, which they had learned of from fellow soldiers who came from farming villages. They also observed how a handful of monopoly capitalists were exploiting the nation for their own profit. It was idealistic patriotism that inspired many of these young officers, but their methods often included assassination, and their fanatical patriotism drove the nation toward war. It is interesting to note that the radical nationalist ideologues Inoue Nisshō (1886–1967) and Kita Ikki (1883–1937), who helped instigate some of the coup attempts, were devout followers of Nichiren, as were some of the young officers involved.

In mobilizing the nation for war the government closely regulated all aspects of Japanese life, including religion. In 1939 it enacted the Religious Organizations Law, which went into effect on April 1, 1940. The law strictly limited the formation of new religious groups and placed existing groups under government control, with religious activities requiring official permission. The new religions were subjected to especially close scrutiny. The Imperial Rule Assistance Association (Taisei Yokusankai), founded in 1940 under government sponsorship, further tightened restrictions on all institutions of Japanese life. The association's policy toward religion was to consolidate groups within each religion.

A few Buddhists did voice opposition to these repressive policies and to the war. The Nichiren follower Seno'o Girō (1889–1961), for example, founded the Dai Nippon Nichirenshugi Seinendan (Great Japan Nichirenist Youth Corps) in 1919. In 1931 this was reorganized as the Shinkō Bukkyō Seinen Dōmei (New Buddhist Youth Alliance). Its members worshiped the historical Buddha, Shakyamuni, aimed to create a Buddhist nation based on brotherly love, and denounced capitalism as anti-Buddhist. The ideal society it envisaged gave central place to the working class. Not surprisingly, this socialist-oriented Buddhist group began to be persecuted by the authorities in the mid-1930s and was finally forced to disband. Meanwhile, as government oppression grew harsher, mainstream Buddhism had all it could do just to survive and capitulated to government control.

It is interesting that followers of Nichiren played such a pivotal role in two opposing groups: patriots, militarists, and right-wing terrorists on the one hand and socialists on the other. Nichiren's teachings, and faith in them, gave strength to both camps. During the war, in fact, several hundred passages were ordered excised from Nichiren's writings, and some followers were imprisoned for lèse-majesté. The two extremes of interpretation that Nichiren's life and thought inspired pose as intriguing a problem as the predominance of Nichiren faith in the Buddhist new religions.

CHAPTER EIGHTEEN

Postwar New Religions and the Future of Buddhism

A S WE HAVE SEEN, the government placed many restrictions on religions before and during World War II. Since the Meiji era Shintō had been under special protection, and its shrines had become symbols of patriotism and reverence for the emperor. In the 1930s Shintō was made a national cult—so-called State Shintō— and adherents of all religions were required to pay homage at Shintō shrines. Since this policy contravened the freedom of religion guaranteed by the Meiji Constitution, the government declared that Shintō was not a religion but an institution presiding over "national rites." As such, it was only natural that the government should extend special protection to it and that adherents of all religions should pay homage at Shintō shrines by virtue of being Japanese.

The government's next step was to bring pressure to bear on any religion that was unwilling to accept its policies, including State Shintō. Most Sectarian Shintō organizations managed to escape persecution, since they worshiped Shintō deities, but Tenrikyō and Konkōkyō were persecuted because their objects of worship did not fit into the official pantheon. Tenri Hommichi, an offshoot of Tenrikyō founded by Ōnishi Aijirō (1881–1958) in 1925, was especially critical of State Shintō. Ōnishi declared himself a living god (*ikigami*), denied the emperor's divinity, and challenged his right to reign. Twice, in 1928 and 1938, Ōnishi was charged with lèse-majesté and arrested. The second time, he was held until the war's end.

As universal religions, Buddhism and Christianity transcended the narrow concerns of the Japanese state. When representatives of these religions criticized the emperor or State Shintō from their broader perspective, they were penalized. For example, Shinran's *Kyō gyō shin shō* states: "When the rulers and their ministers defy the Dharma and violate righteousness, we must be angry and resentful." This and other passages were regarded as provocative and were ordered changed in 1939.

As already mentioned, several hundred passages in Nichiren's writings criticizing the emperor and the Shintō *kami* and challenging their authority were ordered deleted from his collected works in 1941, and in the same year leaders of the Hommon school of the Nichiren sect were arrested in the so-called Mandala Incident. The founder of the Hommon school, Nichiryū (1385–1464), in his commentary on the Mandala of the Ten Realms, identified Amaterasu Ōmikami with the "realms of beasts and demons." This comment, included in a doctrinal text, was noticed by the authorities and led to the charge of lèse-majesté. Christians suffered persecution, too. One of the most difficult tests for Christians was the requirement that all Christian homes and schools have a Shintō altar (*kamidana*). Often they did not, which led of course to persecution.

Shintō-based new religions, unable to obtain official recognition as independent organizations, were relegated to the category of "pseudoreligions" (*ruiji shūkyō*). To continue proselytizing, they affiliated themselves with established Sectarian Shintō or other organizations, but whenever they showed their true character as new religions, the government was quick to slap them down, as we have seen with Ōmoto and Hito no Michi Kyōdan. The new religions, which had such dynamism when they first emerged, were forced to lie low during the war years, but when the war ended they reemerged in a flurry of activity.

On August 15, 1945, Japan surrendered unconditionally to the Allies, and on August 30 General Douglas MacArthur, Supreme

Commander for the Allied Powers, landed at Atsugi Air Base, near Tokyo. SCAP General Headquarters proceeded to disband the Japanese armed forces and eradicate militarism. At the same time, it encouraged a revival of Japanese religions. The first step was the pardon of everyone who had been charged with lèse-majesté. The Religious Organizations Law, which had been the basis for regulating Japanese religious groups, was rescinded and replaced by the Religious Corporations Ordinance on December 28, 1945 (this was superseded by the Religious Corporations Law in 1951).

On December 15, 1945, a directive had been issued forbidding government support of Shintō and removing all militaristic and nationalistic elements from the religion. On January 1, 1946, the emperor publicly denied his divinity, and in November that year a new constitution was promulgated, to go into effect in May 1947. The postwar constitution guaranteed unconditional freedom of religion. For the first time all religious organizations were at liberty to pursue their activities without official interference, and the new religions blossomed in this tolerant climate. The religions founded in the prewar period sprang back to life, and new groups branched off. Reiyūkai, for example, produced Myōchi-kai, Bussho Gonenkai, Myōdō-kai, and Hosshi-kai. (Myōchi-kai, founded by the Reiyūkai member Miyamoto Mitsu [1900–1984] in 1950, remains active today as Myōchi-kai Kyōdan.)

Some bizarre religions were founded, as well. Most soon disappeared, but some, such as the "Dancing Religion" (officially, Tenshō Kōtai Jingūkyō), continued to grow despite criticism and are still active today. The Dancing Religion was founded by Kitamura Sayo (1900–1967), who announced in 1944 that she had received a divine revelation. Upon Japan's defeat she pronounced herself the world's savior, declaring herself the shrine (gū) of the deity Tenshō Kōtaijin, chosen to "drive the maggots from the world" and found a divine kingdom on earth. She also asserted that Nichiren had prophesied her appearance and prescribed a variant of the formula "Namu Myōhō renge kyō" (Hail to the Lotus Sutra) chanted by Nichiren followers. She imparted her teachings, many of which were fantastic or nonsensical, to musical accompaniment, and her followers danced until they were carried away by religious ecstasy. This was called the "dance of selflessness." Her method of proselytization, though it could hardly be called intellectual, attracted a large popular following. Perhaps the most sympathetic of her teachings are ridicule of the powerful and the famous, the conviction that all people are divine children, the desire for world peace, and the founding of a divine kingdom on earth.

Among the Buddhist new religions that have shown the greatest energy since World War II is Sōka Gakkai (Value-Creating Society). First known as Sōka Kyōiku Gakkai (Value-Creating Education Society), it was founded in 1930 by the educator Makiguchi Tsunesaburō (1871–1944). When he was an elementary-school principal, he hired a young teacher named Toda Jōsei (1900–1958), who later became Sōka Gakkai's second president. Makiguchi joined the Nichiren Shōshū sect in 1928, and Toda followed him. Two years later Makiguchi wrote *Sōka kyōikugaku taikei* [The System of Value-Creating Pedagogy] and founded Sōka Kyōiku Gakkai, though its formal inauguration ceremony was not held till 1937.

The membership, mostly elementary-school teachers, grew, and the organization gradually took on more and more of the features of Nichiren Shōshū, becoming a major new religious movement in the process. In 1943, however, when members refused to accept the talismans from Ise Grand Shrine that all households were supposed to enshrine under State Shintō, the organization was persecuted by the authorities, and Makiguchi, Toda, and twenty-one other leaders were arrested. Makiguchi died in prison. Toda was pardoned after the war and revived the organization.

At the first postwar general meeting, held in 1946, the organization's name was changed to Sōka Gakkai. Toda became president in 1951. He promised that his successor would come from the organization's youth division, and sure enough, two years after his death Ikeda Daisaku (1928–), only thirty-two at the time, was chosen as the third president. With the slogan "One truth," Sōka Gakkai launched a vigorous campaign for converts that was espe-

cially effective among young people, who were searching for a focus for their energies and for spiritual support. Ikeda resigned as
president in 1979 (he is now honorary president) and was succeeded
by Hōjō Hiroshi. Hōjō died in 1981, and Akiya Einosuke became
president.

Whether prewar or postwar, Japan's new religions share several
characteristics that can be summed up in three Japanese terms:
okage, tatari, and *naoshi. Okage* is the conviction that religious faith
brings practical benefits in this life, such as cures for illness. The
new religions' emphasis on *okage* no doubt has to do with the
worldly and pragmatic outlook that has typified the Japanese since
ancient times. As pointed out in earlier chapters, the Japanese
have always tended to affirm life; they have rarely rejected the
world or sought to transcend it. The emphasis on the practical in
the new religions thus derives from the national character, which
also helps explain their success. The difficulty that Christianity has
experienced in trying to enlarge its following in Japan can be
traced in part, no doubt, to its otherworldly philosophy, which appeals to few Japanese.

Tatari refers to the malevolent activities of spirits. Many of the
new religions teach that spirits of the dead and other spirits remain active in human affairs and cause mischief unless they are
properly propitiated. The worship of such spirits has persisted in
Japan since ancient times. The teachings of many of the new religions were pronounced by their founders when they felt themselves to be possessed by spirits. This possession is that of the
shaman, who hears the voices of the spirits and conveys their
wishes. Shamanism, too, has colored Japanese political and religious forms since the earliest times.

Reiyūkai and some other new religions place great importance
on veneration of ancestors, which is linked to the centrality of the
clan or family to Japanese life. With the formation of clans in ancient Japan, clan *kami* were created as their symbols and protectors, and the practice of making offerings to ancestors evolved into
ancestor veneration. Ancestor veneration, together with the expec-
tation of practical benefits from religion, is thus characteristic of

Japanese culture, and religions that incorporate these elements are well suited to the Japanese and well received by them.

Naoshi, or renewal, refers to reform of society, to self-renewal, and to improvement of one's life. Most new religions have appeared in periods of social upheaval: times when people's hopes for a better life have been dashed by political and economic trends, times of oppression and dissatisfaction. The new religions have flourished because they offer relief from dissatisfaction.

Many adherents of the new religions are middle-aged women. Some observers have suggested that this reflects the age-old connection between women and shamanism in Japan, but a more likely interpretation is that gatherings of fellow believers provide these women with an outlet for their frustration and dissatisfaction over their limited social role. Male followers tend to come from the lower echelons of society. By joining a religious organization, they can gain the self-esteem denied them by society at large. They gain courage and hope. The organizations, for their part, encourage these feelings and promise that in the future, when the earthly paradise envisioned has been built, their followers will be happy.

The reason most of the Buddhist new religions are based on Nichiren's teachings is that those teachings include elements that correspond to characteristics of the new religions. Nichiren's philosophy emphasizes an active and confrontational attitude toward reality, a critical attitude toward government, a revolutionary social doctrine, a structuralist view of history, a constructive vision of the future, prophecy and admonition, and a spirit of martyrdom.

When we review the ways in which these characteristics manifested themselves over the centuries before the rise of the Nichiren-derived new religions, the first example that comes to mind is the Nichiren faith of the Kyoto *machishū* of the Muromachi period. As discussed in chapter 10, the *machishū* organized themselves into self-governing guilds. At times they even took up arms to protect their interests and their neighborhoods. By about 1400 the Nichiren sect was second only to the Rinzai Zen sect in Kyoto. While the Rinzai sect was supported by the shogunate, it was the capital's *machishū* who supported the Nichiren sect. By 1460 or so most *machishū* were Nichiren followers. The attraction of his teachings for merchants and craftsmen was no doubt his active engagement with reality and his idealism. The livelihood of the *machishū* depended on hard work, positive thinking, and a keen mind and spirit. They saw in Nichiren a kindred soul and in his teachings an inspiring guide.

Nichiren Buddhism also has a tradition of martyrdom, exemplified by the Fuju Fuse subsect. This group shares with Christians the Japanese chapter in the book of martyrdom. The Fuju Fuse martyrs were not restricted to the clergy; women and children also gave their lives for their faith. Perhaps they were able to endure persecution and even death for their beliefs because they shared Nichiren's sense of being a martyred apostle of the truth, of belonging to an embattled spiritual elite.

The Buddhist new religions' emphasis on practical benefits in this life reflects Nichiren's active engagement with reality, while the emphasis on *yo naoshi* derives from his ideal of social reform to create an ideal society, a buddha-land on earth. And the sense of belonging to an elite that characterizes members of the new religions echoes his conviction that he was a messenger of the Buddha. This last is particularly strong in members of Sōka Gakkai and may be one of the reasons it has been so popular among Japanese youth.

In the Meiji era, as we have seen, some thinkers began to link Nichiren's teachings with nationalism. Tanaka Chigaku is perhaps most representative of this type. Militarists and right-wing terrorists like Inoue Nisshō and Kita Ikki were also influenced by that current. Others, however, perceived Nichiren as having placed the authority of the Buddhist Law above the authority of the state. Takayama Chogyū exemplifies this type. These contradictory positions reflect differing interpretations of Nichiren's teaching that the nation must be pacified (*ankoku*) by the establishment of the True Law (*risshō*). Nichiren's teachings were also adopted by some members of the socialist and reformist camp, who saw the spirit of democratic reform in his subordination of state authority to the authority of the Buddhist Law, which led him to criticize the state and counsel reform.

Buddhist temples were meant to be halls of truth, places where the Buddha's teachings are imparted and practiced and centers where those whose lives are sustained by that truth can gather. But in the Edo period temples came to be supported not by individual believers but by the parish, or *danka*, system. Temples became places where memorial services for parishioners' ancestors were held, and this has remained their main function to the present. Buddhist temples in Japan are now primarily cemeteries. The resident priests are custodians of the dead occupied mainly with funerals, death-anniversary services, and festivals of the dead, such as Bon in midsummer and Higan at the spring and autumn equinoxes.

As we have seen, this drastic change in the function of temples in Japanese society occurred soon after the Christian-led Shimabara Uprising of 1637. As part of the Tokugawa shogunate's strategy to eradicate Christianity from Japanese culture, every family was required to register with a temple. The temple register testified to parishioners' religious orthodoxy. This was the origin of the parish system. As long as the temples and their priests participated in this system, they were guaranteed financial support. They soon forgot their duty to minister to the living, since they were guaranteed parishioners, and became the official custodians of the dead.

Of course there were some priests who continued to propagate the Buddha's teachings, and we have already discussed the activities of such Buddhist leaders in the Meiji and Taishō eras. But the majority of Buddhist institutions were satisfied with the easy, established way and did not seek to change it. The Buddhist mainstream supported the Japanese war effort. Only when World War II ended and the parish system was officially abolished was the Buddhist establishment roused from its centuries of torpor.

The new policies that went into effect after the war demolished the base of official support on which the Buddhist establishment had so comfortably rested. For example, land reform greatly reduced temple holdings. It might be expected that this would prompt the temples to revert to their original function of propagating Buddhism, but that did not happen. Land reform simply deprived them of financial security. Freedom of religion liberated temples from the traditional hierarchy of their sects' temple rankings; some temple even severed their sectarian ties. These developments led to considerable acrimony within the Buddhist establishment. All these factors, but especially the dissolution of the parish system, contributed to the temples' increasing financial insecurity. In general, they were at a loss to cope with the situation.

As the Japanese have achieved a high standard of living and considerable material security, however, they have begun to examine their quality of life, and this trend has led to an increased interest in Buddhism. The Buddhist establishment is attempting to respond with new approaches. In addition, Japanese Buddhists are reaching out to Buddhists of other sects and in other countries, and are taking part in joint actions to promote world peace and nuclear disarmament. These developments indicate that the revival of established Japanese Buddhism is possible.

Many of the new religions, meanwhile, have arrived at a crucial stage where they must either adapt or decline, since the circumstances surrounding their inception no longer exist. These religions, having always addressed people's needs directly, have a vigor that established Buddhism lacks. Their peak was the immediate post-war period, when they were able to respond to needs created by the social dislocation and lack of material security that characterized the times. But now that the nation is stable and prosperous and people are focusing on the meaning and purpose of life, religions whose main attraction was the promise of material benefits and those that attracted followers with emotional and dramatic methods of propagation unsupported by profound teachings are finding themselves at a difficult turning point.

Of course there are still people in Japan who lack material comforts or can be moved by emotional appeals, but the general trend is toward an increased interest in philosophies and religions that offer a deeper interpretation of life. The new religions that can devise methods of propagation to meet this need are likely to continue to grow and develop, while those that cannot do so will either stagnate or decline. The time has come for the new religions to establish more sophisticated doctrinal systems while taking care to preserve their freshness of approach. That is the key to their continued growth.

This has been called the age of alienation. People have lost sight of the meaning of life. They are in search of spiritual sustenance. At times this search reaches such a degree of frustration that it explodes in bizarre ways. This is the danger of our age. How to cope with this danger is the challenge facing both established Buddhism and the new religions.

Index